On
Leadership for Healthcare

HBR's 10 Must Reads series is the definitive collection of ideas and best practices for aspiring and experienced leaders alike. These books offer essential reading selected from the pages of *Harvard Business Review* on topics critical to the success of every manager.

Titles include:

On Leadership for Healthcare

HARVARD BUSINESS REVIEW PRESS
Boston, Massachusetts

Copyright 2018 Harvard Business School Publishing Corporation
All rights reserved
Printed in the United States of America
10 9 8 7 6 5 4

No part of this publication may be reproduced, stored in or introduced into a retrieval system, or transmitted, in any form, or by any means (electronic, mechanical, photocopying, recording, or otherwise), without the prior permission of the publisher. Requests for permission should be directed to permissions@hbsp.harvard.edu, or mailed to Permissions, Harvard Business School Publishing, 60 Harvard Way, Boston, Massachusetts 02163.

The web addresses referenced in this book were live and correct at the time of the book's publication but may be subject to change.

Library of Congress Cataloging-in-Publication Data

Title: HBR's 10 must reads on leadership for healthcare.
Other titles: HBR's 10 must reads (Series)
Description: Boston, Massachusetts : Harvard Business Review Press, [2018] | Series: HBR's 10 must reads
Identifiers: LCCN 2017059593 | ISBN 9781633694323 (pbk.)
Subjects: LCSH: Health services administration. | Leadership.
Classification: LCC RA971 .H38315 2018 | DDC 362.1068—dc23 LC record available at https://lccn.loc.gov/2017059593

The paper used in this publication meets the requirements of the American National Standard for Permanence of Paper for Publications and Documents in Libraries and Archives Z39.48-1992.

ISBN: 9781633694323
eISBN: 9781633694330

Contents

Introduction

by Thomas H. Lee

Over the last half century, for the CEOs and senior managers of health care organizations, the meaning of leadership has gone through two transformations. In the kinder, gentler past, financial pressures were mild, and quality was considered unmeasurable. In the absence of compelling metrics for "output" or pressures to contain costs, business success depended on preserving relationships, brand building, and crisis management, and these were the skills prized in health care leaders.

The surge in medical progress that began in the 1960s, which resulted from increased investments in research in the years after World War II, drove the first transformation away from this status quo. Untreatable diseases became treatable, and some even became curable. For example, innovations like coronary artery bypass graft surgery, coronary angioplasty, thrombolysis, and statins for cholesterol reduction transformed cardiology from a passive to an active discipline. Almost every area of medicine had analogous advances.

Before these advances, medicine had been a field in which physicians made diagnoses, predicted prognoses, and relieved suffering. But now, health care providers could actually change the future, often for the better, and sometimes for the worse. There were many more medications and operations that might help patients live better and longer lives, but occasionally the wrong drug was given, and procedures went awry. As medicine became more active, the safety and quality of care began to attract more attention, and health care leaders have had to learn the skills needed to improve them within their organizations—like measuring data and organizing personnel to reliably perform at their best.

And it turns out that improving care is different work from keeping the peace. Leaders must be willing to enter into conflicts and manage them well. They must excel at negotiation. Simultaneously, they must have empathy for their patients, and, as in any business sector, they must deploy emotional intelligence to broker good relationships with their personnel. That work is especially complex with physicians and nurses, who are rightly proud of their professional standing and the quality of their work.

The second transformation in health care leadership has come in response to the other side of the equation from patient outcomes: costs. Health care spending rose about 2.5% per year faster than the growth of the rest of the economy after 1970, accounting for an increasing share of the U.S. economy. The federal government started to try to apply the brakes on spending with the Balanced Budget Act of 1997, which cut payments to doctors and hospitals. For a time, providers were able to get increases from commercial insurers that made up for the lower payment rates for Medicare and Medicaid payments, but those times have come to an end. Instead, leaders must learn to make the difficult strategic decisions—and to understand the efficiency of the operations behind them—in order to contain costs.

These two transformations mean that today's health care CEOs and C-suite teams face pressures to improve quality *and* costs. These leaders must broker complex relationships while simultaneously driving improvement in performance. For health care leaders, these roles require a special mix of soft and hard skills. Health care executives need to lead change management in organizational cultures that have traditionally celebrated autonomy. They need to understand the difference between leadership and management, and bridge the gap between them—keeping an eye on the horizon as well as the dangers in the waters immediately before them. They need to build real teams that work together to improve quality and efficiency, without losing the intense individual motivations that draw people into health care.

The need for improvement in performance has also meant that senior executives in health care have to define their organization's culture, orienting it around a clear purpose and shared values. The leaders themselves must "walk the walk" of those values. And words and phrases that have been rhetorical flourishes—like "improvement," "high reliability," "trust," "teamwork," and "resilience"—are now operational imperatives.

To help health care leaders improve performance, this volume of Must Read articles collects *Harvard Business Review*'s definitive articles on leadership in any sector, as well as some pieces chosen specifically for a health care readership.

The collection begins with four landmark *Harvard Business Review* articles on the nature of leadership and the makeup of leaders. Daniel Goleman defines the aspects of emotional intelligence that are core competencies for leaders, including empathy, which has moved from a "nice to have" to a "must have" for executives as well as clinicians in health care. Peter Drucker's foundational thinking on the role of a leader shows how leadership and management practices exist on a spectrum; they are not separate types of work for separate people. John Kotter's treatise on change management is a nice complement to this way of thinking in that it offers another perspective on the differences between leadership and management, even while providing a framework for how leaders can drive change in their organizations. Jim Collins's article defining "Level 5 Leadership" provides a description of what it means to put all these elements together in a package that enables a leader to take an organization through challenge and change.

The other articles we've included address some of the special challenges for leaders in health care in today's era. Ronald Heifetz and Donald Laurie's article on "The Work of Leadership" describes how leadership in times of turmoil requires more than having a vision and aligning a workforce; they offer key principles for how leaders should create a context for change. Amy Edmondson's article "Teamwork on the Fly" acknowledges both the importance of teamwork and the reality that teams often have to be pulled together for special initiatives—like the care of a complex patient. That means that leaders need to develop the skills to inspire and enable this quick ability to form teams on the fly—what she calls "teaming"—that can become a critical competitive differentiator for providers.

Paul Rogers and Marcia Blenko's article "Who Has the D?" touches a sensitive nerve in a lot of health care organizations, where it often seems that *no one* has clear decision-making rights and responsibilities. This article offers leaders a solid framework for determining and communicating which decisions get made by whom.

Deborah Ancona and her colleagues acknowledge that no one has all the skills to do everything expected from the leader of an organization with complex functions—like so many of those in the health care sector. Instead, they describe how leaders can build a "distributed leadership" model that spreads key skills, tasks, and functions, and doesn't unrealistically ask any one person to do everything.

Robert Kaplan and David Norton's article on using the balanced scorecard is critical reading for leaders who understand that they must also manage.

And the last two articles, which more deliberately address the health care sector, describe some of the specifics of what elements of the organization a health care leader must manage and how they can involve clinicians in that work.

We have chosen these articles because, collectively, they help define the range of skills and perspectives that are essential for leading complex work through times of change, with increasing pressures from a marketplace that demands improvement in both quality and efficiency. We offer them with full awareness that health care *is* a special sector, with unusually high stakes for its personnel and its patient-customers. But there are nevertheless valuable lessons for health care leaders from the other business sectors, especially as health care grows more strategic, cost aware, and patient focused. The insights from this collection can enable health care leaders to better understand the skills they need for their most important work.

What Makes a Leader?

by Daniel Goleman

EVERY BUSINESSPERSON KNOWS a story about a highly intelligent, highly skilled executive who was promoted into a leadership position only to fail at the job. And they also know a story about someone with solid—but not extraordinary—intellectual abilities and technical skills who was promoted into a similar position and then soared.

Such anecdotes support the widespread belief that identifying individuals with the "right stuff" to be leaders is more art than science. After all, the personal styles of superb leaders vary: Some leaders are subdued and analytical; others shout their manifestos from the mountaintops. And just as important, different situations call for different types of leadership. Most mergers need a sensitive negotiator at the helm, whereas many turnarounds require a more forceful authority.

I have found, however, that the most effective leaders are alike in one crucial way: They all have a high degree of what has come to be known as *emotional intelligence*. It's not that IQ and technical skills are irrelevant. They do matter, but mainly as "threshold capabilities"; that is, they are the entry-level requirements for executive positions. But my research, along with other recent studies, clearly shows that emotional intelligence is the sine qua non of leadership. Without it, a person can have the best training in the world, an incisive, analytical mind, and an endless supply of smart ideas, but he still won't make a great leader.

A Bit of Context

Every important measure of performance—financial margin, through-put (for example, average length of a patient's stay), safety, patient experience—has been shown to correlate with the pride that doctors, nurses, and other personnel feel in their organization, and the confidence that their organization is committed to core values like quality and safety. Shared values are particularly important during times of transition, like the overhaul that health care is experiencing. Organizations are merging, care is being redesigned, and payment models are being turned on their heads. As a result, health care leaders must not only clearly communicate shared organizational values, but also demonstrate that these values are fundamental for them personally.

Doing so takes emotional intelligence as psychologist Dan Goleman has defined it in this landmark article. Health care leaders need the self-awareness to understand how they are perceived and to make themselves visible—out on the floors of hospitals and clinics, for example. They need the discipline to be unwavering in their embrace of the core values of their profession and the empathy to understand the impact of change and pressure on their personnel. And they have to ask questions, listen, and tell stories that demonstrate that they really do embrace those values throughout their work. Leaders also need the social skills to get clinicians and others to build their own strong values and live into them reliably. Health care is a relationship-based business, and its leaders must have real relationships with their colleagues that inspire trust, respect, and cooperation.

The material in this article will be familiar to many readers, but its inclusion in this book is a reminder that everyone can get better at all five of Goleman's elements of emotional intelligence: self-awareness, self-regulation, motivation, empathy, and social skill. In doing so, health care leaders will have a better chance at motivating their teams to take on challenging or new work.

—Thomas H. Lee

In the course of the past year, my colleagues and I have focused on how emotional intelligence operates at work. We have examined the relationship between emotional intelligence and effective performance, especially in leaders. And we have observed how emotional intelligence shows itself on the job. How can you tell if

Idea in Brief

What distinguishes great leaders from merely good ones? It isn't IQ or technical skills, says Daniel Goleman. It's **emotional intelligence:** a group of five skills that enable the best leaders to maximize their own *and* their followers' performance. When senior managers at one company had a critical mass of EI capabilities, their divisions outperformed yearly earnings goals by 20%.

The EI skills are:

- *Self-awareness*—knowing one's strengths, weaknesses, drives, values, and impact on others

- *Self-regulation*—controlling or redirecting disruptive impulses and moods

- *Motivation*—relishing achievement for its own sake

- *Empathy*—understanding other people's emotional makeup

- *Social skill*—building rapport with others to move them in desired directions

We're each born with certain levels of EI skills. But we can strengthen these abilities through persistence, practice, and feedback from colleagues or coaches.

someone has high emotional intelligence, for example, and how can you recognize it in yourself? In the following pages, we'll explore these questions, taking each of the components of emotional intelligence—self-awareness, self-regulation, motivation, empathy, and social skill—in turn.

Evaluating Emotional Intelligence

Most large companies today have employed trained psychologists to develop what are known as "competency models" to aid them in identifying, training, and promoting likely stars in the leadership firmament. The psychologists have also developed such models for lower-level positions. And in recent years, I have analyzed competency models from 188 companies, most of which were large and global and included the likes of Lucent Technologies, British Airways, and Credit Suisse.

In carrying out this work, my objective was to determine which personal capabilities drove outstanding performance within these organizations, and to what degree they did so. I grouped capabilities

Idea in Practice

Understanding EI's Components

EI Component	Definition	Hallmarks	Example
Self-awareness	Knowing one's emotions, strengths, weaknesses, drives, values, and goals—and their impact on others	• Self-confidence • Realistic self-assessment • Self-deprecating sense of humor • Thirst for constructive criticism	A manager knows tight deadlines bring out the worst in him. So he plans his time to get work done well in advance.
Self-regulation	Controlling or redirecting disruptive emotions and impulses	• Trustworthiness • Integrity • Comfort with ambiguity and change	When a team botches a presentation, its leader resists the urge to scream. Instead, she considers possible reasons for the failure, explains the consequences to her team, and explores solutions with them.
Motivation	Being driven to achieve for the sake of achievement	• A passion for the work itself and for new challenges • Unflagging energy to improve • Optimism in the face of failure	A portfolio manager at an investment company sees his fund tumble for three consecutive quarters. Major clients defect. Instead of blaming external circumstances, she decides to learn from the experience—and engineers a turn-around.

Empathy	Considering others' feelings, especially when making decisions	• Expertise in attracting and retaining talent • Ability to develop others • Sensitivity to cross-cultural differences	An American consultant and her team pitch a project to a potential client in Japan. Her team interprets the client's silence as disapproval, and prepares to leave. The consultant reads the client's body language and senses interest. She continues the meeting, and her team gets the job.
Social skill	Managing relationships to move people in desired directions	• Effectiveness in leading change • Persuasiveness • Extensive networking • Expertise in building and leading teams	A manager wants his company to adopt a better Internet strategy. He finds kindred spirits and assembles a de facto team to create a prototype Web site. He persuades allies in other divisions to fund the company's participation in a relevant convention. His company forms an Internet division—and puts him in charge of it.

Strengthening Your EI

Use practice and feedback from others to strengthen specific EI skills.

Example: An executive learned from others that she lacked empathy, especially the ability to listen. She wanted to fix the problem, so she asked a coach to tell her when she exhibited poor listening skills. She then role-played incidents to practice giving better responses; for example, not interrupting. She also began observing executives skilled at listening—and imitated their behavior.

The five components of emotional intelligence at work

	Definition	Hallmarks
Self-awareness	The ability to recognize and understand your moods, emotions, and drives, as well as their effect on others	Self-confidence Realistic self-assessment Self-deprecating sense of humor
Self-regulation	The ability to control or redirect disruptive impulses and moods The propensity to suspend judgment—to think before acting	Trustworthiness and integrity Comfort with ambiguity Openness to change
Motivation	A passion to work for reasons that go beyond money or status A propensity to pursue goals with energy and persistence	Strong drive to achieve Optimism, even in the face of failure Organizational commitment
Empathy	The ability to understand the emotional makeup of other people Skill in treating people according to their emotional reactions	Expertise in building and retaining talent Cross-cultural sensitivity Service to clients and customers
Social skill	Proficiency in managing relationships and building networks An ability to find common ground and build rapport	Effectiveness in leading change Persuasiveness Expertise in building and leading teams

into three categories: purely technical skills like accounting and business planning; cognitive abilities like analytical reasoning; and competencies demonstrating emotional intelligence, such as the ability to work with others and effectiveness in leading change.

To create some of the competency models, psychologists asked senior managers at the companies to identify the capabilities that typified the organization's most outstanding leaders. To create other models, the psychologists used objective criteria, such as a division's profitability, to differentiate the star performers at senior levels within their organizations from the average ones. Those individuals were then extensively interviewed and tested, and their capabilities were compared. This process resulted in the creation of lists of ingredients for highly effective leaders. The lists ranged in length from seven to 15 items and included such ingredients as initiative and strategic vision.

When I analyzed all this data, I found dramatic results. To be sure, intellect was a driver of outstanding performance. Cognitive skills such as big-picture thinking and long-term vision were particularly important. But when I calculated the ratio of technical skills, IQ, and emotional intelligence as ingredients of excellent performance, emotional intelligence proved to be twice as important as the others for jobs at all levels.

Moreover, my analysis showed that emotional intelligence played an increasingly important role at the highest levels of the company, where differences in technical skills are of negligible importance. In other words, the higher the rank of a person considered to be a star performer, the more emotional intelligence capabilities showed up as the reason for his or her effectiveness. When I compared star performers with average ones in senior leadership positions, nearly 90% of the difference in their profiles was attributable to emotional intelligence factors rather than cognitive abilities.

Other researchers have confirmed that emotional intelligence not only distinguishes outstanding leaders but can also be linked to strong performance. The findings of the late David McClelland, the renowned researcher in human and organizational behavior, are a good example. In a 1996 study of a global food and beverage

7

company, McClelland found that when senior managers had a critical mass of emotional intelligence capabilities, their divisions outperformed yearly earnings goals by 20%. Meanwhile, division leaders without that critical mass underperformed by almost the same amount. McClelland's findings, interestingly, held as true in the company's U.S. divisions as in its divisions in Asia and Europe.

In short, the numbers are beginning to tell us a persuasive story about the link between a company's success and the emotional intelligence of its leaders. And just as important, research is also demonstrating that people can, if they take the right approach, develop their emotional intelligence. (See the sidebar "Can Emotional Intelligence Be Learned?")

Self-Awareness

Self-awareness is the first component of emotional intelligence—which makes sense when one considers that the Delphic oracle gave the advice to "know thyself" thousands of years ago. Self-awareness means having a deep understanding of one's emotions, strengths, weaknesses, needs, and drives. People with strong self-awareness are neither overly critical nor unrealistically hopeful. Rather, they are honest—with themselves and with others.

People who have a high degree of self-awareness recognize how their feelings affect them, other people, and their job performance. Thus, a self-aware person who knows that tight deadlines bring out the worst in him plans his time carefully and gets his work done well in advance. Another person with high self-awareness will be able to work with a demanding client. She will understand the client's impact on her moods and the deeper reasons for her frustration. "Their trivial demands take us away from the real work that needs to be done," she might explain. And she will go one step further and turn her anger into something constructive.

Self-awareness extends to a person's understanding of his or her values and goals. Someone who is highly self-aware knows where he is headed and why; so, for example, he will be able to be firm in turning down a job offer that is tempting financially but does not fit with his principles or long-term goals. A person who lacks self-awareness is apt to make decisions that bring on inner turmoil by treading on buried values. "The money looked good so I signed on," someone might say two years into a job, "but the work means so little to me that I'm constantly bored." The decisions of self-aware people mesh with their values; consequently, they often find work to be energizing.

How can one recognize self-awareness? First and foremost, it shows itself as candor and an ability to assess oneself realistically. People with high self-awareness are able to speak accurately and openly—although not necessarily effusively or confessionally—about their emotions and the impact they have on their work. For instance, one manager I know of was skeptical about a new personal-shopper service that her company, a major department-store chain, was about to introduce. Without prompting from her team or her boss, she offered them an explanation: "It's hard for me to get behind the rollout of this service," she admitted, "because I really wanted to run the project, but I wasn't selected. Bear with me while I deal with that." The manager did indeed examine her feelings; a week later, she was supporting the project fully.

Such self-knowledge often shows itself in the hiring process. Ask a candidate to describe a time he got carried away by his feelings and did something he later regretted. Self-aware candidates will be frank in admitting to failure—and will often tell their tales with a smile. One of the hallmarks of self-awareness is a self-deprecating sense of humor.

Self-awareness can also be identified during performance reviews. Self-aware people know—and are comfortable talking about—their limitations and strengths, and they often demonstrate a thirst for constructive criticism. By contrast, people with low self-awareness interpret the message that they need to improve as a threat or a sign of failure.

Self-aware people can also be recognized by their self-confidence. They have a firm grasp of their capabilities and are less likely to set themselves up to fail by, for example, overstretching on assignments. They know, too, when to ask for help. And the risks they take on the job are calculated. They won't ask for a challenge that they know they can't handle alone. They'll play to their strengths.

Can Emotional Intelligence Be Learned?

FOR AGES, PEOPLE HAVE DEBATED if leaders are born or made. So too goes the debate about emotional intelligence. Are people born with certain levels of empathy, for example, or do they acquire empathy as a result of life's experiences? The answer is both. Scientific inquiry strongly suggests that there is a genetic component to emotional intelligence. Psychological and developmental research indicates that nurture plays a role as well. How much of each perhaps will never be known, but research and practice clearly demonstrate that emotional intelligence can be learned.

One thing is certain: Emotional intelligence increases with age. There is an old-fashioned word for the phenomenon: maturity. Yet even with maturity, some people still need training to enhance their emotional intelligence. Unfortunately, far too many training programs that intend to build leadership skills—including emotional intelligence—are a waste of time and money. The problem is simple: They focus on the wrong part of the brain.

Emotional intelligence is born largely in the neurotransmitters of the brain's limbic system, which governs feelings, impulses, and drives. Research indicates that the limbic system learns best through motivation, extended practice, and feedback. Compare this with the kind of learning that goes on in the neocortex, which governs analytical and technical ability. The neocortex grasps concepts and logic. It is the part of the brain that figures out how to use a computer or make a sales call by reading a book. Not surprisingly—but mistakenly—it is also the part of the brain targeted by most training programs aimed at enhancing emotional intelligence. When such programs take, in effect, a neocortical approach, my research with the Consortium for Research on Emotional Intelligence in Organizations has shown they can even have a *negative* impact on people's job performance.

To enhance emotional intelligence, organizations must refocus their training to include the limbic system. They must help people break old behavioral habits and establish new ones. That not only takes much more time than conventional training programs, it also requires an individualized approach.

Imagine an executive who is thought to be low on empathy by her colleagues. Part of that deficit shows itself as an inability to listen; she interrupts people and doesn't pay close attention to what they're saying. To fix the problem, the executive needs to be motivated to change, and then she needs practice and feedback from others in the company. A colleague or coach could be tapped to let the executive know when she has been observed failing to listen. She would then have to replay the incident and give a better response; that is, demonstrate her ability to absorb what others are saying. And the executive could be directed to observe certain executives who listen well and to mimic their behavior.

With persistence and practice, such a process can lead to lasting results. I know one Wall Street executive who sought to improve his empathy—specifically his ability to read people's reactions and see their perspectives. Before beginning his quest, the executive's subordinates were terrified of working with him. People even went so far as to hide bad news from him. Naturally, he was shocked when finally confronted with these facts. He went home and told his family—but they only confirmed what he had heard at work. When their opinions on any given subject did not mesh with his, they, too, were frightened of him.

Enlisting the help of a coach, the executive went to work to heighten his empathy through practice and feedback. His first step was to take a vacation to a foreign country where he did not speak the language. While there, he monitored his reactions to the unfamiliar and his openness to people who were different from him. When he returned home, humbled by his week abroad, the executive asked his coach to shadow him for parts of the day, several times a week, to critique how he treated people with new or different perspectives. At the same time, he consciously used on-the-job interactions as opportunities to practice "hearing" ideas that differed from his. Finally, the executive had himself videotaped in meetings and asked those who worked for and with him to critique his ability to acknowledge and understand the feelings of others. It took several months, but the executive's emotional intelligence did ultimately rise, and the improvement was reflected in his overall performance on the job.

It's important to emphasize that building one's emotional intelligence cannot—will not—happen without sincere desire and concerted effort. A brief seminar won't help; nor can one buy a how-to manual. It is much harder to learn to empathize—to internalize empathy as a natural response to people—than it is to become adept at regression analysis. But it can be done. "Nothing great was ever achieved without enthusiasm," wrote Ralph Waldo Emerson. If your goal is to become a real leader, these words can serve as a guidepost in your efforts to develop high emotional intelligence.

Consider the actions of a midlevel employee who was invited to sit in on a strategy meeting with her company's top executives. Although she was the most junior person in the room, she did not sit there quietly, listening in awestruck or fearful silence. She knew she had a head for clear logic and the skill to present ideas persuasively, and she offered cogent suggestions about the company's strategy. At the same time, her self-awareness stopped her from wandering into territory where she knew she was weak.

Despite the value of having self-aware people in the workplace, my research indicates that senior executives don't often give self-awareness the credit it deserves when they look for potential leaders. Many executives mistake candor about feelings for "wimpiness" and fail to give due respect to employees who openly acknowledge their shortcomings. Such people are too readily dismissed as "not tough enough" to lead others.

In fact, the opposite is true. In the first place, people generally admire and respect candor. Furthermore, leaders are constantly required to make judgment calls that require a candid assessment of capabilities—their own and those of others. Do we have the management expertise to acquire a competitor? Can we launch a new product within six months? People who assess themselves honestly—that is, self-aware people—are well suited to do the same for the organizations they run.

Self-Regulation

Biological impulses drive our emotions. We cannot do away with them—but we can do much to manage them. Self-regulation, which is like an ongoing inner conversation, is the component of emotional intelligence that frees us from being prisoners of our feelings. People engaged in such a conversation feel bad moods and emotional impulses just as everyone else does, but they find ways to control them and even to channel them in useful ways.

Imagine an executive who has just watched a team of his employees present a botched analysis to the company's board of directors. In the gloom that follows, the executive might find himself tempted to pound on the table in anger or kick over a chair. He could leap up and scream at the group. Or he might maintain a grim silence, glaring at everyone before stalking off.

But if he had a gift for self-regulation, he would choose a different approach. He would pick his words carefully, acknowledging the team's poor performance without rushing to any hasty judgment. He would then step back to consider the reasons for the failure. Are they personal—a lack of effort? Are there any mitigating factors? What was his role in the debacle? After considering these questions, he would call the team together, lay out the incident's consequences, and offer his feelings about it. He would then present his analysis of the problem and a well-considered solution.

Why does self-regulation matter so much for leaders? First of all, people who are in control of their feelings and impulses—that is, people who are reasonable—are able to create an environment of trust and fairness. In such an environment, politics and infighting are sharply reduced and productivity is high. Talented people flock to the organization and aren't tempted to leave. And self-regulation has a trickle-down effect. No one wants to be known as a hothead when the boss is known for her calm approach. Fewer bad moods at the top mean fewer throughout the organization.

Second, self-regulation is important for competitive reasons. Everyone knows that business today is rife with ambiguity and change. Companies merge and break apart regularly. Technology transforms work at a dizzying pace. People who have mastered their emotions are able to roll with the changes. When a new program is announced, they don't panic; instead, they are able to suspend judgment, seek out information, and listen to the executives as they explain the new program. As the initiative moves forward, these people are able to move with it.

Sometimes they even lead the way. Consider the case of a manager at a large manufacturing company. Like her colleagues, she had used a certain software program for five years. The program drove how she collected and reported data and how she thought about the company's strategy. One day, senior executives announced that a new program was to be installed that would radically change how information was gathered and assessed within the organization. While many people in the company complained bitterly about how disruptive the change would be, the manager mulled over the reasons for the new program and was convinced of its potential to improve performance. She eagerly attended training sessions—some of her colleagues refused to do so—and was eventually promoted to run several divisions, in part because she used the new technology so effectively.

I want to push the importance of self-regulation to leadership even further and make the case that it enhances integrity, which is not only a personal virtue but also an organizational strength. Many of the bad things that happen in companies are a function of impulsive behavior. People rarely plan to exaggerate profits, pad expense accounts, dip into the till, or abuse power for selfish ends. Instead, an opportunity presents itself, and people with low impulse control just say yes.

By contrast, consider the behavior of the senior executive at a large food company. The executive was scrupulously honest in his negotiations with local distributors. He would routinely lay out his cost structure in detail, thereby giving the distributors a realistic understanding of the company's pricing. This approach meant the executive couldn't always drive a hard bargain. Now, on occasion, he felt the urge to increase profits by withholding information about the company's costs. But he challenged that impulse—he saw that it made more sense in the long run to counteract it. His emotional self-regulation paid off in strong, lasting relationships with distributors that benefited the company more than any short-term financial gains would have.

The signs of emotional self-regulation, therefore, are easy to see: a propensity for reflection and thoughtfulness; comfort with ambiguity and change; and integrity—an ability to say no to impulsive urges.

Like self-awareness, self-regulation often does not get its due. People who can master their emotions are sometimes seen as cold fish—their considered responses are taken as a lack of passion. People with fiery temperaments are frequently thought of as "classic" leaders—their outbursts are considered hallmarks of charisma and power. But when such people make it to the top, their impulsiveness often works against them. In my research, extreme displays of negative emotion have never emerged as a driver of good leadership.

Motivation

If there is one trait that virtually all effective leaders have, it is motivation. They are driven to achieve beyond expectations—their own and everyone else's. The key word here is *achieve*. Plenty of people are motivated by external factors, such as a big salary or the status that comes from having an impressive title or being part of a prestigious company. By contrast, those with leadership potential are motivated by a deeply embedded desire to achieve for the sake of achievement.

If you are looking for leaders, how can you identify people who are motivated by the drive to achieve rather than by external rewards? The first sign is a passion for the work itself—such people seek out creative challenges, love to learn, and take great pride in a job well done. They also display an unflagging energy to do things better. People with such energy often seem restless with the status quo. They are persistent with their questions about why things are done one way rather than another; they are eager to explore new approaches to their work.

A cosmetics company manager, for example, was frustrated that he had to wait two weeks to get sales results from people in the field. He finally tracked down an automated phone system that would beep each of his salespeople at 5 PM every day. An automated message then prompted them to punch in their numbers—how many calls and sales they had made that day. The system shortened the feedback time on sales results from weeks to hours.

That story illustrates two other common traits of people who are driven to achieve. They are forever raising the performance bar, and they like to keep score. Take the performance bar first. During performance reviews, people with high levels of motivation might ask to be "stretched" by their superiors. Of course, an employee who combines self-awareness with internal motivation will recognize her limits—but she won't settle for objectives that seem too easy to fulfill.

And it follows naturally that people who are driven to do better also want a way of tracking progress—their own, their team's, and their company's. Whereas people with low achievement motivation are often fuzzy about results, those with high achievement motivation often keep score by tracking such hard measures as profitability or market share. I know of a money manager who starts and ends his day on the Internet, gauging the performance of his stock fund against four industry-set benchmarks.

Interestingly, people with high motivation remain optimistic even when the score is against them. In such cases, self-regulation combines with achievement motivation to overcome the frustration and depression that come after a setback or failure. Take the case of another portfolio manager at a large investment company. After several successful years, her fund tumbled for three consecutive quarters, leading three large institutional clients to shift their business elsewhere.

Some executives would have blamed the nosedive on circumstances outside their control; others might have seen the setback as evidence of personal failure. This portfolio manager, however, saw an opportunity to prove she could lead a turnaround. Two years later, when she was promoted to a very senior level in the company, she described the experience as "the best thing that ever happened to me; I learned so much from it."

Executives trying to recognize high levels of achievement motivation in their people can look for one last piece of evidence: commitment to the organization. When people love their jobs for the work itself, they often feel committed to the organizations that make that work possible. Committed employees are likely to stay with an organization even when they are pursued by headhunters waving money.

It's not difficult to understand how and why a motivation to achieve translates into strong leadership. If you set the performance bar high for yourself, you will do the same for the organization when you are in a position to do so. Likewise, a drive to surpass goals and an interest in keeping score can be contagious. Leaders with these traits can often build a team of managers around them with the same traits. And of course, optimism and organizational commitment are fundamental to leadership—just try to imagine running a company without them.

Empathy

Of all the dimensions of emotional intelligence, empathy is the most easily recognized. We have all felt the empathy of a sensitive teacher or friend; we have all been struck by its absence in an unfeeling coach or boss. But when it comes to business, we rarely hear people praised, let alone rewarded, for their empathy. The very word seems unbusinesslike, out of place amid the tough realities of the marketplace.

But empathy doesn't mean a kind of "I'm OK, you're OK" mushiness. For a leader, that is, it doesn't mean adopting other people's emotions as one's own and trying to please everybody. That would be a nightmare—it would make action impossible. Rather, empathy means thoughtfully considering employees' feelings—along with other factors—in the process of making intelligent decisions.

For an example of empathy in action, consider what happened when two giant brokerage companies merged, creating redundant jobs in all their divisions. One division manager called his people together and gave a gloomy speech that emphasized the number of people who would soon be fired. The manager of another division gave his people a different kind of speech. He was up-front about his own worry and confusion, and he promised to keep people informed and to treat everyone fairly.

The difference between these two managers was empathy. The first manager was too worried about his own fate to consider the feelings of his anxiety-stricken colleagues. The second knew intuitively what his people were feeling, and he acknowledged their fears with his words. Is it any surprise that the first manager saw his division sink as many demoralized people, especially the most talented, departed? By contrast, the second manager continued to be a strong leader, his best people stayed, and his division remained as productive as ever.

Empathy is particularly important today as a component of leadership for at least three reasons: the increasing use of teams; the rapid pace of globalization; and the growing need to retain talent.

Consider the challenge of leading a team. As anyone who has ever been a part of one can attest, teams are cauldrons of bubbling emotions. They are often charged with reaching a consensus—which is hard enough with two people and much more difficult as the numbers increase. Even in groups with as few as four or five members, alliances form and clashing agendas get set. A team's leader must be able to sense and understand the viewpoints of everyone around the table.

That's exactly what a marketing manager at a large information technology company was able to do when she was appointed to lead a troubled team. The group was in turmoil, overloaded by work and missing deadlines. Tensions were high among the members. Tinkering with procedures was not enough to bring the group together and make it an effective part of the company.

So the manager took several steps. In a series of one-on-one sessions, she took the time to listen to everyone in the group—what was frustrating them, how they rated their colleagues, whether they felt they had been ignored. And then she directed the team in a way that brought it together: She encouraged people to speak more openly about their frustrations, and she helped people raise constructive complaints during meetings. In short, her empathy allowed her to understand her team's emotional makeup. The result was not just heightened collaboration among members but also added business, as the team was called on for help by a wider range of internal clients.

Globalization is another reason for the rising importance of empathy for business leaders. Cross-cultural dialogue can easily lead to miscues and misunderstandings. Empathy is an antidote. People who have it are attuned to subtleties in body language; they can hear the message beneath the words being spoken. Beyond that, they have a deep understanding of both the existence and the importance of cultural and ethnic differences.

Consider the case of an American consultant whose team had just pitched a project to a potential Japanese client. In its dealings with Americans, the team was accustomed to being bombarded with questions after such a proposal, but this time it was greeted with a long silence. Other members of the team, taking the silence as disapproval, were ready to pack and leave. The lead consultant gestured them to stop. Although he was not particularly familiar with Japanese culture, he read the client's face and posture and sensed not rejection but interest—even deep consideration. He was right: When the client finally spoke, it was to give the consulting firm the job.

Finally, empathy plays a key role in the retention of talent, particularly in today's information economy. Leaders have always needed empathy to develop and keep good people, but today the stakes are higher. When good people leave, they take the company's knowledge with them.

That's where coaching and mentoring come in. It has repeatedly been shown that coaching and mentoring pay off not just in better performance but also in increased job satisfaction and decreased turnover. But what makes coaching and mentoring work best is the nature of the relationship. Outstanding coaches and mentors get inside the heads of the people they are helping. They sense how to give effective feedback. They know when to push for better performance and when to hold back. In the way they motivate their protégés, they demonstrate empathy in action.

In what is probably sounding like a refrain, let me repeat that empathy doesn't get much respect in business. People wonder how leaders can make hard decisions if they are "feeling" for all the people who will be affected. But leaders with empathy do more than sympathize with people around them: They use their knowledge to improve their companies in subtle but important ways.

Social Skill

The first three components of emotional intelligence are self-management skills. The last two, empathy and social skill, concern a person's ability to manage relationships with others. As a component of emotional intelligence, social skill is not as simple as it sounds. It's not just a matter of friendliness, although people with high levels of social skill are rarely mean-spirited. Social skill, rather, is friendliness with a purpose: moving people in the direction you desire, whether that's agreement on a new marketing strategy or enthusiasm about a new product.

Socially skilled people tend to have a wide circle of acquaintances, and they have a knack for finding common ground with people of all kinds—a knack for building rapport. That doesn't mean they socialize continually; it means they work according to the assumption that nothing important gets done alone. Such people have a network in place when the time for action comes.

Social skill is the culmination of the other dimensions of emotional intelligence. People tend to be very effective at managing relationships when they can understand and control their own emotions and can empathize with the feelings of others. Even motivation contributes to social skill. Remember that people who are driven to achieve tend to be optimistic, even in the face of setbacks or failure. When people are upbeat, their "glow" is cast upon conversations and other social encounters. They are popular, and for good reason.

Because it is the outcome of the other dimensions of emotional intelligence, social skill is recognizable on the job in many ways that will by now sound familiar. Socially skilled people, for instance, are adept at managing teams—that's their empathy at work. Likewise, they are expert persuaders—a manifestation of self-awareness, self-regulation, and empathy combined. Given those skills, good persuaders know when to make an emotional plea, for instance, and when an appeal to reason will work better. And motivation, when publicly visible, makes such people excellent collaborators; their passion for the work spreads to others, and they are driven to find solutions.

But sometimes social skill shows itself in ways the other emotional intelligence components do not. For instance, socially skilled people may at times appear not to be working while at work. They seem to be idly schmoozing—chatting in the hallways with colleagues or joking around with people who are not even connected to their "real" jobs.

Socially skilled people, however, don't think it makes sense to arbitrarily limit the scope of their relationships. They build bonds widely because they know that in these fluid times, they may need help someday from people they are just getting to know today.

For example, consider the case of an executive in the strategy department of a global computer manufacturer. By 1993, he was convinced that the company's future lay with the Internet. Over the course of the next year, he found kindred spirits and used his social skill to stitch together a virtual community that cut across levels, divisions, and nations. He then used this de facto team to put up a corporate Web site, among the first by a major company. And, on his own initiative, with no budget or formal status, he signed up the company to participate in an annual Internet industry convention. Calling on his allies and persuading various divisions to donate funds, he recruited more than 50 people from a dozen different units to represent the company at the convention.

Management took notice: Within a year of the conference, the executive's team formed the basis for the company's first Internet division, and he was formally put in charge of it. To get there, the executive had ignored conventional boundaries, forging and maintaining connections with people in every corner of the organization.

Is social skill considered a key leadership capability in most companies? The answer is yes, especially when compared with the other components of emotional intelligence. People seem to know intuitively that leaders need to manage relationships effectively; no leader is an island. After all, the leader's task is to get work done through other people, and social skill makes that possible. A leader who cannot express her empathy may as well not have it at all. And a leader's motivation will be useless if he cannot communicate his passion to the organization. Social skill allows leaders to put their emotional intelligence to work.

It would be foolish to assert that good-old-fashioned IQ and technical ability are not important ingredients in strong leadership. But the recipe would not be complete without emotional intelligence. It was once thought that the components of emotional intelligence were "nice to have" in business leaders. But now we know that, for the sake of performance, these are ingredients that leaders "need to have."

It is fortunate, then, that emotional intelligence can be learned. The process is not easy. It takes time and, most of all, commitment. But the benefits that come from having a well-developed emotional intelligence, both for the individual and for the organization, make it worth the effort.

Originally published in June 1996. Reprint R0401H

What Makes an Effective Executive

by Peter F. Drucker

AN EFFECTIVE EXECUTIVE DOES NOT need to be a leader in the sense that the term is now most commonly used. Harry Truman did not have one ounce of charisma, for example, yet he was among the most effective chief executives in U.S. history. Similarly, some of the best business and nonprofit CEOs I've worked with over a 65-year consulting career were not stereotypical leaders. They were all over the map in terms of their personalities, attitudes, values, strengths, and weaknesses. They ranged from extroverted to nearly reclusive, from easygoing to controlling, from generous to parsimonious.

What made them all effective is that they followed the same eight practices:

- They asked, "What needs to be done?"

- They asked, "What is right for the enterprise?"

- They developed action plans.

- They took responsibility for decisions.

- They took responsibility for communicating.

- They were focused on opportunities rather than problems.

- They ran productive meetings.

- They thought and said "we" rather than "I."

The first two practices gave them the knowledge they needed. The next four helped them convert this knowledge into effective action. The last two ensured that the whole organization felt responsible and accountable.

Get the Knowledge You Need

The first practice is to ask what needs to be done. Note that the question is not "What do I want to do?" Asking what has to be done, and taking the question seriously, is crucial for managerial success. Failure to ask this question will render even the ablest executive ineffectual.

When Truman became president in 1945, he knew exactly what he wanted to do: complete the economic and social reforms of Roosevelt's New Deal, which had been deferred by World War II. As soon as he asked what needed to be done, though, Truman realized that foreign affairs had absolute priority. He organized his working day so that it began with tutorials on foreign policy by the secretaries of state and defense. As a result, he became the most effective president in foreign affairs the United States has ever known. He contained Communism in both Europe and Asia and, with the Marshall Plan, triggered 50 years of worldwide economic growth.

Similarly, Jack Welch realized that what needed to be done at General Electric when he took over as chief executive was not the overseas expansion he wanted to launch. It was getting rid of GE businesses that, no matter how profitable, could not be number one or number two in their industries.

The answer to the question "What needs to be done?" almost always contains more than one urgent task. But effective executives do not splinter themselves. They concentrate on one task if at all possible. If they are among those people—a sizable minority—who work best with a change of pace in their working day, they pick two tasks. I have never encountered an executive who remains effective while tackling more than two tasks at a time. Hence, after asking what needs to be done, the effective executive sets priorities and sticks to them. For a CEO, the priority task might be redefining

Idea in Brief

Worried that you're not a born leader? That you lack charisma, the right talents, or some other secret ingredient? No need: leadership isn't about personality or talent. In fact, the best leaders exhibit wildly different personalities, attitudes, values, and strengths—they're extroverted or reclusive, easygoing or controlling, generous or parsimonious, numbers or vision oriented.

So what do effective leaders have in common? They get the right things done, in the right ways—by following eight simple rules:

- Ask what needs to be done.
- Ask what's right for the enterprise.
- Develop action plans.
- Take responsibility for decisions.
- Take responsibility for communicating.
- Focus on opportunities, not problems.
- Run productive meetings.
- Think and say "we," not "I."

Using discipline to apply these rules, you gain the knowledge you need to make smart decisions, convert that knowledge into effective action, and ensure accountability throughout your organization.

---

the company's mission. For a unit head, it might be redefining the unit's relationship with headquarters. Other tasks, no matter how important or appealing, are postponed. However, after completing the original top-priority task, the executive resets priorities rather than moving on to number two from the original list. He asks, "What must be done now?" This generally results in new and different priorities.

To refer again to America's best-known CEO: Every five years, according to his autobiography, Jack Welch asked himself, "What needs to be done *now?*" And every time, he came up with a new and different priority.

But Welch also thought through another issue before deciding where to concentrate his efforts for the next five years. He asked himself which of the two or three tasks at the top of the list he himself was best suited to undertake. Then he concentrated on that task; the others he delegated. Effective executives try to focus on jobs

Idea in Practice

Get the Knowledge You Need

Ask what needs to be done. When Jack Welch asked this question while taking over as CEO at General Electric, he realized that dropping GE businesses that couldn't be first or second in their industries was essential—not the overseas expansion he had wanted to launch. Once you know what must be done, identify tasks you're best at, concentrating on one at a time. After completing a task, reset priorities based on new realities.

Ask what's right for the enterprise. Don't agonize over what's best for owners, investors, employees, or customers. Decisions that are right for your *enterprise* are ultimately right for all stakeholders.

Convert Your Knowledge into Action

Develop action plans. Devise plans that specify *desired results* and *constraints* (Is the course of action legal and compatible with the company's mission, values, and policies?). Include *check-in points* and *implications for how you'll spend your time*. And *revise* plans to reflect new opportunities.

Take responsibility for decisions. Ensure that each decision specifies who's accountable for carrying it out, when it must be implemented, who'll be affected by it, and who must be informed. Regularly review decisions, especially hires and promotions. This enables you to correct poor decisions before doing real damage.

Take responsibility for communicating. Get input from superiors, subordinates, and peers on your action plans. Let each know what information you need to get the job done. Pay equal attention to

they'll do especially well. They know that enterprises perform if top management performs—and don't if it doesn't.

Effective executives' second practice—fully as important as the first—is to ask, "Is this the right thing for the enterprise?" They do not ask if it's right for the owners, the stock price, the employees, or the executives. Of course they know that shareholders, employees, and executives are important constituencies who have to support a decision, or at least acquiesce in it, if the choice is to be effective. They know that the share price is important not only for the shareholders but also for the enterprise, since the price/earnings ratio sets the cost of capital. But they also know that a decision that isn't right for the enterprise will ultimately not be right for any of the stakeholders.

WHAT MAKES AN EFFECTIVE EXECUTIVE

peers' and superiors' information needs.

Focus on opportunities, not problems. You get results by exploiting opportunities, not solving problems. Identify changes inside and outside your organization (new technologies, product innovations, new market structures), asking "How can we exploit this change to benefit our enterprise?" Then match your best people with the best opportunities.

Ensure Companywide Accountability

Run productive meetings. Articulate each meeting's purpose (Making an announcement? Delivering a report?). Terminate the meeting once the purpose is accomplished. Follow up with short communications summarizing the discussion, spelling out new work assignments and deadlines for completing them. General Motors CEO Alfred Sloan's legendary mastery of meeting follow-up helped secure GM's industry dominance in the mid-twentieth century.

Think and say "we," not "I." Your authority comes from your organization's trust in you. To get the best results, always consider your organization's needs and opportunities before your own.

This second practice is especially important for executives at family owned or family run businesses—the majority of businesses in every country—particularly when they're making decisions about people. In the successful family company, a relative is promoted only if he or she is measurably superior to all nonrelatives on the same level. At DuPont, for instance, all top managers (except the controller and lawyer) were family members in the early years when the firm was run as a family business. All male descendants of the founders were entitled to entry-level jobs at the company. Beyond the entrance level, a family member got a promotion only if a panel composed primarily of nonfamily managers judged the person to be superior in ability and performance to all other employees at the same level. The same rule was observed for a century in the highly successful British family business J. Lyons & Company (now part of a major conglomerate) when it dominated the British food-service and hotel industries.

Asking "What is right for the enterprise?" does not guarantee that the right decision will be made. Even the most brilliant executive is human and thus prone to mistakes and prejudices. But failure to ask the question virtually guarantees the *wrong* decision.

Write an Action Plan

Executives are doers; they execute. Knowledge is useless to executives until it has been translated into deeds. But before springing into action, the executive needs to plan his course. He needs to think about desired results, probable restraints, future revisions, check-in points, and implications for how he'll spend his time.

First, the executive defines desired results by asking: "What contributions should the enterprise expect from me over the next 18 months to two years? What results will I commit to? With what deadlines?" Then he considers the restraints on action: "Is this course of action ethical? Is it acceptable within the organization? Is it legal? Is it compatible with the mission, values, and policies of the organization?" Affirmative answers don't guarantee that the action will be effective. But violating these restraints is certain to make it both wrong and ineffectual.

The action plan is a statement of intentions rather than a commitment. It must not become a straitjacket. It should be revised often, because every success creates new opportunities. So does every failure. The same is true for changes in the business environment, in the market, and especially in people within the enterprise—all these changes demand that the plan be revised. A written plan should anticipate the need for flexibility.

In addition, the action plan needs to create a system for checking the results against the expectations. Effective executives usually build two such checks into their action plans. The first check comes halfway through the plan's time period; for example, at nine months. The second occurs at the end, before the next action plan is drawn up.

Finally, the action plan has to become the basis for the executive's time management. Time is an executive's scarcest and most precious resource. And organizations—whether government agencies, businesses, or nonprofits—are inherently time wasters. The action plan will prove useless unless it's allowed to determine how the executive spends his or her time.

Napoleon allegedly said that no successful battle ever followed its plan. Yet Napoleon also planned every one of his battles, far more meticulously than any earlier general had done. Without an action plan, the executive becomes a prisoner of events. And without check-ins to reexamine the plan as events unfold, the executive has no way of knowing which events really matter and which are only noise.

Act

When they translate plans into action, executives need to pay particular attention to decision making, communication, opportunities (as opposed to problems), and meetings. I'll consider these one at a time.

Take responsibility for decisions

A decision has not been made until people know:

- the name of the person accountable for carrying it out;

- the deadline;

- the names of the people who will be affected by the decision and therefore have to know about, understand, and approve it—or at least not be strongly opposed to it—and

- the names of the people who have to be informed of the decision, even if they are not directly affected by it.

An extraordinary number of organizational decisions run into trouble because these bases aren't covered. One of my clients, 30 years ago, lost its leadership position in the fast-growing Japanese market because the company, after deciding to enter into a joint venture with a new Japanese partner, never made clear who was to inform the purchasing agents that the partner defined its specifications in meters and kilograms rather than feet and pounds—and nobody ever did relay that information.

It's just as important to review decisions periodically—at a time that's been agreed on in advance—as it is to make them carefully in the first place. That way, a poor decision can be corrected before it does real damage. These reviews can cover anything from the results to the assumptions underlying the decision.

Such a review is especially important for the most crucial and most difficult of all decisions, the ones about hiring or promoting people. Studies of decisions about people show that only one-third of such choices turn out to be truly successful. One-third are likely to be draws—neither successes nor outright failures. And one-third are failures, pure and simple. Effective executives know this and check up (six to nine months later) on the results of their people decisions. If they find that a decision has not had the desired results, they don't conclude that the person has not performed. They conclude, instead, that they themselves made a mistake. In a well-managed enterprise, it is understood that people who fail in a new job, especially after a promotion, may not be the ones to blame.

Executives also owe it to the organization and to their fellow workers not to tolerate nonperforming individuals in important jobs. It may not be the employees' fault that they are underperforming, but even so, they have to be removed. People who have failed in a new job should be given the choice to go back to a job at their former level and salary. This option is rarely exercised; such people, as a rule, leave voluntarily, at least when their employers are U.S. firms. But the very existence of the option can have a powerful effect, encouraging people to leave safe, comfortable jobs and take risky new assignments. The organization's performance depends on employees' willingness to take such chances.

A systematic decision review can be a powerful tool for self-development, too. Checking the results of a decision against its expectations shows executives what their strengths are, where they need to improve, and where they lack knowledge or information. It shows them their biases. Very often it shows them that their decisions didn't produce results because they didn't put the right people on the job. Allocating the best people to the right positions is a crucial, tough job that many executives slight, in part because the best people are already too busy. Systematic decision review also shows executives their own weaknesses, particularly the areas in which they are simply incompetent. In these areas, smart executives don't make decisions or take actions. They delegate. Everyone has such areas; there's no such thing as a universal executive genius.

Most discussions of decision making assume that only senior executives make decisions or that only senior executives' decisions matter. This is a dangerous mistake. Decisions are made at every level of the organization, beginning with individual professional contributors and frontline supervisors. These apparently low-level decisions are extremely important in a knowledge-based organization. Knowledge workers are supposed to know more about their areas of specialization—for example, tax accounting—than anybody else, so their decisions are likely to have an impact throughout the company. Making good decisions is a crucial skill at every level. It needs to be taught explicitly to everyone in organizations that are based on knowledge.

Take responsibility for communicating

Effective executives make sure that both their action plans and their information needs are understood. Specifically, this means that they share their plans with and ask for comments from all their colleagues—superiors, subordinates, and peers. At the same time, they let each person know what information they'll need to get the job done. The information flow from subordinate to boss is usually what gets the most attention. But executives need to pay equal attention to peers' and superiors' information needs.

We all know, thanks to Chester Barnard's 1938 classic *The Functions of the Executive,* that organizations are held together by information rather than by ownership or command. Still, far too many executives behave as if information and its flow were the job of the information specialist—for example, the accountant. As a result, they get an enormous amount of data they do not need and cannot use, but little of the information they do need. The best way around this problem is for each executive to identify the information he needs, ask for it, and keep pushing until he gets it.

Focus on opportunities

Good executives focus on opportunities rather than problems. Problems have to be taken care of, of course; they must not be swept under the rug. But problem solving, however necessary, does not produce results. It prevents damage. Exploiting opportunities produces results.

Above all, effective executives treat change as an opportunity rather than a threat. They systematically look at changes, inside and outside the corporation, and ask, "How can we exploit this change as an opportunity for our enterprise?" Specifically, executives scan these seven situations for opportunities:

- an unexpected success or failure in their own enterprise, in a competing enterprise, or in the industry;

- a gap between what is and what could be in a market, process, product, or service (for example, in the nineteenth century, the paper industry concentrated on the 10% of each tree that became wood pulp and totally neglected the possibilities in the remaining 90%, which became waste);

- innovation in a process, product, or service, whether inside or outside the enterprise or its industry;

- changes in industry structure and market structure;

- demographics;

- changes in mind-set, values, perception, mood, or meaning; and

- new knowledge or a new technology.

Effective executives also make sure that problems do not overwhelm opportunities. In most companies, the first page of the monthly management report lists key problems. It's far wiser to list opportunities on the first page and leave problems for the second page. Unless there is a true catastrophe, problems are not discussed in management meetings until opportunities have been analyzed and properly dealt with.

Staffing is another important aspect of being opportunity focused. Effective executives put their best people on opportunities rather than on problems. One way to staff for opportunities is to ask each member of the management group to prepare two lists every six months—a list of opportunities for the entire enterprise and a list of the best-performing people throughout the enterprise. These are discussed, then melded into two master lists, and the best people are matched with the best opportunities. In Japan, by the way, this matchup is considered a major HR task in a big corporation or government department; that practice is one of the key strengths of Japanese business.

Make meetings productive

The most visible, powerful, and, arguably, effective nongovernmental executive in the America of World War II and the years thereafter was not a businessman. It was Francis Cardinal Spellman, the head of the Roman Catholic Archdiocese of New York and adviser to several U.S. presidents. When Spellman took over, the diocese was bankrupt and totally demoralized. His successor inherited the leadership position in the American Catholic church. Spellman often said that during his waking hours he was alone only twice each day, for 25 minutes each time: when he said Mass in his private chapel after getting up in the morning and when he said his evening prayers before going to bed. Otherwise he was always with people in a meeting, starting at breakfast with one Catholic organization and ending at dinner with another.

Top executives aren't quite as imprisoned as the archbishop of a major Catholic diocese. But every study of the executive workday has found that even junior executives and professionals are with other people—that is, in a meeting of some sort—more than half of every business day. The only exceptions are a few senior researchers. Even a conversation with only one other person is a meeting. Hence, if they are to be effective, executives must make meetings productive. They must make sure that meetings are work sessions rather than bull sessions.

The key to running an effective meeting is to decide in advance what kind of meeting it will be. Different kinds of meetings require different forms of preparation and different results.

A meeting to prepare a statement, an announcement, or a press release. For this to be productive, one member has to prepare a draft beforehand. At the meeting's end, a preappointed member has to take responsibility for disseminating the final text.

A meeting to make an announcement—for example, an organizational change. This meeting should be confined to the announcement and a discussion about it.

A meeting in which one member reports. Nothing but the report should be discussed.

A meeting in which several or all members report. Either there should be no discussion at all or the discussion should be limited to questions for clarification. Alternatively, for each report there could be a short discussion in which all participants may ask questions. If this is the format, the reports should be distributed to all participants well before the meeting. At this kind of meeting, each report should be limited to a preset time—for example, 15 minutes.

A meeting to inform the convening executive. The executive should listen and ask questions. He or she should sum up but not make a presentation.

A meeting whose only function is to allow the participants to be in the executive's presence. Cardinal Spellman's breakfast and dinner meetings were of that kind. There is no way to make these meetings productive. They are the penalties of rank. Senior executives are effective to the extent to which they can prevent such meetings from encroaching on their workdays. Spellman, for instance, was effective in large part because he confined such meetings to break-fast and dinner and kept the rest of his working day free of them.

Making a meeting productive takes a good deal of self-discipline. It requires that executives determine what kind of meeting is appropriate and then stick to that format. It's also necessary to terminate the meeting as soon as its specific purpose has been accomplished. Good executives don't raise another matter for discussion. They sum up and adjourn.

Good follow-up is just as important as the meeting itself. The great master of follow-up was Alfred Sloan, the most effective business executive I have ever known. Sloan, who headed General Motors from the 1920s until the 1950s, spent most of his six working days a week in meetings—three days a week in formal committee meetings with a set membership, the other three days in ad hoc meetings with individual GM executives or with a small group of executives. At the beginning of a formal meeting, Sloan announced the meeting's purpose. He then listened. He never took notes and he rarely spoke except to clarify a confusing point. At the end he summed up, thanked the participants, and left. Then he immediately wrote a short memo addressed to one attendee of the meeting. In that note, he summarized the discussion and its conclusions and spelled out any work assignment decided upon in the meeting (including a decision to hold another meeting on the subject or to study an issue). He specified the deadline and the executive who was to be accountable for the assignment. He sent a copy of the memo to everyone who'd been present at the meeting. It was through these memos—each a small masterpiece—that Sloan made himself into an outstandingly effective executive.

Effective executives know that any given meeting is either productive or a total waste of time.

Think and Say "We"

The final practice is this: Don't think or say "I." Think and say "we." Effective executives know that they have ultimate responsibility, which can be neither shared nor delegated. But they have authority only because they have the trust of the organization. This means that they think of the needs and the opportunities of the organization before they think of their own needs and opportunities. This one may sound simple; it isn't, but it needs to be strictly observed.

We've just reviewed eight practices of effective executives. I'm going to throw in one final, bonus practice. This one's so important that I'll elevate it to the level of a rule: *Listen first, speak last.*

Effective executives differ widely in their personalities, strengths, weaknesses, values, and beliefs. All they have in common is that they get the right things done. Some are born effective. But the demand is much too great to be satisfied by extraordinary talent. Effectiveness is a discipline. And, like every discipline, effectiveness *can* be learned and *must* be earned.

Originally published in June 2004. Reprint R0406C

What Leaders Really Do

by John P. Kotter

LEADERSHIP IS DIFFERENT FROM MANAGEMENT, but not for the reasons most people think. Leadership isn't mystical and mysterious. It has nothing to do with having "charisma" or other exotic personality traits. It is not the province of a chosen few. Nor is leadership necessarily better than management or a replacement for it.

Rather, leadership and management are two distinctive and complementary systems of action. Each has its own function and characteristic activities. Both are necessary for success in an increasingly complex and volatile business environment.

Most U.S. corporations today are over-managed and underled. They need to develop their capacity to exercise leadership. Successful corporations don't wait for leaders to come along. They actively seek out people with leadership potential and expose them to career experiences designed to develop that potential. Indeed, with careful selection, nurturing, and encouragement, dozens of people can play important leadership roles in a business organization.

But while improving their ability to lead, companies should remember that strong leadership with weak management is no better, and is sometimes actually worse, than the reverse. The real challenge is to combine strong leadership and strong management and use each to balance the other.

Of course, not everyone can be good at both leading and managing. Some people have the capacity to become excellent managers

A Bit of Context

In the health care sector, paths to leadership are often unplanned and unexpected. Many leaders, for example, are doctors or nurses who rose to strategic positions because of the respect and trust they earned through years of research or excellent clinical care. These technical skills and the deep understanding of health care practice that come with them are valuable for health care leaders because their colleagues know that they grasp the demands and complexity of clinical work and have paid their dues.

But these clinician-leaders have not always developed or appreciated skills in bread-and-butter management, such as running meetings, developing a budget and then sticking to it, and overseeing operations. Similarly, nonclinicians who have made their way to senior roles in health care organizations because of their effectiveness in management must learn to appreciate the idiosyncrasies and distinguishing features of the culture of health care organizations in order to lead them well.

This article by John Kotter crystallizes these categories of "leadership" and "management," defining management as being about coping with complexity, and leadership as about coping with change. Kotter suggests that organizations need both and shows how the same person can develop both approaches.

These categories should resonate with health care leaders, because health care has plenty of both change and complexity. For example, organizations need leadership to avoid getting paralyzed by exceptions, such as an unusual patient for whom routine protocols might be harmful. They need management to ensure that the protocols are reliably used to make care better and more efficient for the typical patient. And—particularly during a time of market change and pressures for performance—they need integration of leadership and management to ensure that those protocols have the flexibility to detect and adjust for that exceptional patient for whom they should not be applied.

The stories in this article are from corporations like American Express, Eastman Kodak, and Procter & Gamble, but if you focus on the kinds of work that the leaders do—setting direction, aligning people, and motivating people, for example—you'll see connections with leadership and management in health care.

—Thomas H. Lee

Idea in Brief

The most pernicious half-truth about leadership is that it's just a matter of charisma and vision—you either have it or you don't. The fact of the matter is that leadership skills are not innate. They can be acquired, and honed. But first you have to appreciate how they differ from management skills.

Management is about coping with *complexity*; it brings order and predictability to a situation. But that's no longer enough—to succeed, companies must be able to adapt to change. Leadership, then,

is about learning how to cope with rapid *change*.

How does this distinction play out?

- Management involves planning and budgeting. Leadership involves setting direction.

- Management involves organizing and staffing. Leadership involves aligning people.

- Management provides control and solves problems. Leadership provides motivation.

but not strong leaders. Others have great leadership potential but, for a variety of reasons, have great difficulty becoming strong managers. Smart companies value both kinds of people and work hard to make them a part of the team.

But when it comes to preparing people for executive jobs, such companies rightly ignore the recent literature that says people cannot manage *and* lead. They try to develop leader-managers. Once companies understand the fundamental difference between leadership and management, they can begin to groom their top people to provide both.

The Difference Between Management and Leadership

Management is about coping with complexity. Its practices and procedures are largely a response to one of the most significant developments of the twentieth century: the emergence of large organizations. Without good management, complex enterprises tend to become chaotic in ways that threaten their very existence. Good management brings a degree of order and consistency to key dimensions like the quality and profitability of products.

Idea in Practice

Management and leadership both involve deciding what needs to be done, creating networks of people to accomplish the agenda, and ensuring that the work actually gets done. Their work is complementary, but each system of action goes about the tasks in different ways.

1. Planning and budgeting versus setting direction. The aim of management is predictability—orderly results. Leadership's function is to produce change. Setting the direction of that change, therefore, is essential work. There's nothing mystical about this work, but it is more inductive than planning and budgeting. It involves the search for patterns and relationships. And it doesn't produce detailed plans; instead, direction-setting results in visions and the overarching strategies for realizing them.

> *Example:* In mature industries, increased competition usually dampens growth. But at American Express, Lou Gerstner bucked this trend, successfully crafting a vision of a dynamic enterprise.

> The new direction he set wasn't a mere attention-grabbing scheme—it was the result of asking fundamental questions about market and competitive forces.

2. Organizing and staffing versus aligning people. Managers look for the right fit between people and jobs. This is essentially a design problem: setting up systems to ensure that plans are implemented precisely and efficiently. Leaders, however, look for the right fit between people and the vision. This is more of a communication problem. It involves getting a large number of people, inside and outside the company, first to believe in an alternative future—and then to take initiative based on that shared vision.

3. Controlling activities and solving problems versus motivating and inspiring. Management strives to make it easy for people to complete routine jobs day after day. But since high energy is essential to overcoming the barriers to change, leaders attempt to touch people at their deepest levels—by stirring in them a sense of belonging, idealism, and self-esteem.

> *Example:* At Procter & Gamble's paper products division, Richard Nicolosi underscored the message that "each of us is a leader" by pushing responsibility down to newly formed teams. An entrepreneurial attitude took root, and profits rebounded.

Leadership, by contrast, is about coping with change. Part of the reason it has become so important in recent years is that the business world has become more competitive and more volatile. Faster technological change, greater international competition, the deregulation of markets, overcapacity in capital-intensive industries, an unstable oil cartel, raiders with junk bonds, and the changing demographics of the work-force are among the many factors that have contributed to this shift. The net result is that doing what was done yesterday, or doing it 5% better, is no longer a formula for success. Major changes are more and more necessary to survive and compete effectively in this new environment. More change always demands more leadership.

Consider a simple military analogy: A peacetime army can usually survive with good administration and management up and down the hierarchy, coupled with good leadership concentrated at the very top. A wartime army, however, needs competent leadership at all levels. No one yet has figured out how to manage people effectively into battle; they must be led.

These two different functions—coping with complexity and coping with change—shape the characteristic activities of management and leadership. Each system of action involves deciding what needs to be done, creating networks of people and relationships that can accomplish an agenda, and then trying to ensure that those people actually do the job. But each accomplishes these three tasks in different ways.

Companies manage complexity first by *planning and budgeting*—setting targets or goals for the future (typically for the next month or year), establishing detailed steps for achieving those targets, and then allocating resources to accomplish those plans. By contrast, leading an organization to constructive change begins by *setting a direction*—developing a vision of the future (often the distant future) along with strategies for producing the changes needed to achieve that vision.

Management develops the capacity to achieve its plan by *organizing and staffing*—creating an organizational structure and set of jobs for accomplishing plan requirements, staffing the jobs with qualified individuals, communicating the plan to those people, delegating responsibility for carrying out the plan, and devising systems to monitor implementation. The equivalent leadership activity, however, is *aligning people*. This means communicating the new direction to those who can create coalitions that understand the vision and are committed to its achievement.

Finally, management ensures plan accomplishment by *controlling and problem solving*—monitoring results versus the plan in some detail, both formally and informally, by means of reports, meetings, and other tools; identifying deviations; and then planning and organizing to solve the problems. But for leadership, achieving a vision requires *motivating and inspiring*—keeping people moving in the right direction, despite major obstacles to change, by appealing to basic but often untapped human needs, values, and emotions.

A closer examination of each of these activities will help clarify the skills leaders need.

Setting a Direction Versus Planning and Budgeting

Since the function of leadership is to produce change, setting the direction of that change is fundamental to leadership. Setting direction is never the same as planning or even long-term planning, although people often confuse the two. Planning is a management process, deductive in nature and designed to produce orderly results, not change. Setting a direction is more inductive. Leaders gather a broad range of data and look for patterns, relationships, and linkages that help explain things. What's more, the direction-setting aspect of leadership does not produce plans; it creates vision and strategies. These describe a business, technology, or corporate culture in terms of what it should become over the long term and articulate a feasible way of achieving this goal.

Most discussions of vision have a tendency to degenerate into the mystical. The implication is that a vision is something mysterious that mere mortals, even talented ones, could never hope to have. But developing good business direction isn't magic. It is a tough, sometimes exhausting process of gathering and analyzing information.

People who articulate such visions aren't magicians but broad-based strategic thinkers who are willing to take risks.

Nor do visions and strategies have to be brilliantly innovative; in fact, some of the best are not. Effective business visions regularly have an almost mundane quality, usually consisting of ideas that are already well known. The particular combination or patterning of the ideas may be new, but sometimes even that is not the case.

For example, when CEO Jan Carlzon articulated his vision to make Scandinavian Airlines System (SAS) the best airline in the world for the frequent business traveler, he was not saying anything that everyone in the airline industry didn't already know. Business travelers fly more consistently than other market segments and are generally willing to pay higher fares. Thus, focusing on business customers offers an airline the possibility of high margins, steady business, and considerable growth. But in an industry known more for bureaucracy than vision, no company had ever put these simple ideas together and dedicated itself to implementing them. SAS did, and it worked.

What's crucial about a vision is not its originality but how well it serves the interests of important constituencies—customers, stockholders, employees—and how easily it can be translated into a realistic competitive strategy. Bad visions tend to ignore the legitimate needs and rights of important constituencies—favoring, say, employees over customers or stockholders. Or they are strategically unsound. When a company that has never been better than a weak competitor in an industry suddenly starts talking about becoming number one, that is a pipe dream, not a vision.

One of the most frequent mistakes that overmanaged and underled corporations make is to embrace long-term planning as a panacea for their lack of direction and inability to adapt to an increasingly competitive and dynamic business environment. But such an approach misinterprets the nature of direction setting and can never work.

Long-term planning is always time consuming. Whenever something unexpected happens, plans have to be redone. In a dynamic business environment, the unexpected often becomes the norm, and long-term planning can become an extraordinarily burdensome activity. That is why most successful corporations limit the

Aligning People: Chuck Trowbridge and Bob Crandall at Eastman Kodak

EASTMAN KODAK ENTERED THE copy business in the early 1970s, concentrating on technically sophisticated machines that sold, on average, for about $60,000 each. Over the next decade, this business grew to nearly $1 billion in revenues. But costs were high, profits were hard to find, and problems were nearly everywhere. In 1984, Kodak had to write off $40 million in inventory. Most people at the company knew there were problems, but they couldn't agree on how to solve them. So in his first two months as general manager of the new copy products group, established in 1984, Chuck Trowbridge met with nearly every key person inside his group, as well as with people elsewhere at Kodak who could be important to the copier business. An especially crucial area was the engineering and manufacturing organization, headed by Bob Crandall.

Trowbridge and Crandall's vision for engineering and manufacturing was simple: to become a world-class manufacturing operation and to create a less bureaucratic and more decentralized organization. Still, this message was difficult to convey because it was such a radical departure from previous communications, not only in the copy products group but throughout most of Kodak. So Crandall set up dozens of vehicles to emphasize the new direction and align people to it: weekly meetings with his own 12 direct reports; monthly "copy product forums" in which a different employee from each of his departments would meet with him as a group; discussions of recent improvements and new projects to achieve still better results; and quarterly "State of the Department" meetings, where his managers met with everybody in their own departments.

Once a month, Crandall and all those who reported to him would also meet with 80 to 100 people from some area of his organization to discuss anything

time frame of their planning activities. Indeed, some even consider "long-term planning" a contradiction in terms.

In a company without direction, even short-term planning can become a black hole capable of absorbing an infinite amount of time and energy. With no vision and strategy to provide constraints around the planning process or to guide it, every eventuality deserves a plan. Under these circumstances, contingency planning can go on forever, draining time and attention from far more essential activities, yet without ever providing the clear sense of direction they wanted. To align his biggest supplier—the Kodak Apparatus Division, which supplied one-third of the parts used in design and manufacturing—he and his managers met with the top management of that group over lunch every Thursday. Later, he created a format called "business meetings," where his managers meet with 12 to 20 people on a specific topic, such as inventory or master scheduling. The goal: to get all of his 1,500 employees in at least one of these focused business meetings each year.

Trowbridge and Crandall also enlisted written communication in their cause. A four- to eight-page "Copy Products Journal" was sent to employees once a month. A program called "Dialog Letters" gave employees the opportunity to anonymously ask questions of Crandall and his top managers and be guaranteed a reply. But the most visible and powerful written communications were the charts. In a main hallway near the cafeteria, these huge charts vividly reported the quality, cost, and delivery results for each product, measured against difficult targets. A hundred smaller versions of these charts were scattered throughout the manufacturing area, reporting quality levels and costs for specific work groups.

Results of this intensive alignment process began to appear within six months, and still more surfaced after a year. These successes made the message more credible and helped get more people on board. Between 1984 and 1988, quality on one of the main product lines increased nearly 100-fold. Defects per unit went from 30 to 0.3. Over a three-year period, costs on another product line went down nearly 24%. Deliveries on schedule increased from 82% in 1985 to 95% in 1987. Inventory levels dropped by over 50% between 1984 and 1988, even though the volume of products was increasing. And productivity, measured in units per manufacturing employee, more than doubled between 1985 and 1988.

that a company desperately needs. After awhile, managers inevitably become cynical, and the planning process can degenerate into a highly politicized game.

Planning works best not as a substitute for direction setting but as a complement to it. A competent planning process serves as a useful reality check on direction-setting activities. Likewise, a competent direction-setting process provides a focus in which planning can then be realistically carried out. It helps clarify what kind of planning is essential and what kind is irrelevant.

Setting a Direction: Lou Gerstner at American Express

WHEN LOU GERSTNER BECAME PRESIDENT of the Travel Related Services (TRS) arm at American Express in 1979, the unit was facing one of its biggest challenges in AmEx's 130-year history. Hundreds of banks offering or planning to introduce credit cards through Visa and MasterCard that would compete with the American Express card. And more than two dozen financial service firms were coming into the traveler's checks business. In a mature marketplace, this increase in competition usually reduces margins and prohibits growth.

But that was not how Gerstner saw the business. Before joining American Express, he had spent five years as a consultant to TRS, analyzing the money-losing travel division and the increasingly competitive card operation. Gerstner and his team asked fundamental questions about the economics, market, and competition and developed a deep understanding of the business. In the process, he began to craft a vision of TRS that looked nothing like a 130-year-old company in a mature industry.

Gerstner thought TRS had the potential to become a dynamic and growing enterprise, despite the onslaught of Visa and MasterCard competition from thousands of banks. The key was to focus on the global marketplace and, specifically, on the relatively affluent customer American Express had been traditionally serving with top-of-the-line products. By further segmenting this market, aggressively developing a broad range of new products and services, and investing to increase productivity and to lower costs, TRS could provide the best service possible to customers who had enough discretionary income to buy many more services from TRS than they had in the past.

Within a week of his appointment, Gerstner brought together the people running the card organization and questioned all the principles by which they conducted their business. In particular, he challenged two widely shared beliefs—that the division should have only one product, the green card, and that this product was limited in potential for growth and innovation.

Aligning People Versus Organizing and Staffing

A central feature of modern organizations is interdependence, where no one has complete autonomy, where most employees are tied to many others by their work, technology, management systems, and hierarchy. These linkages present a special challenge

Gerstner also moved quickly to develop a more entrepreneurial culture, to hire and train people who would thrive in it, and to clearly communicate to them the overall direction. He and other top managers rewarded intelligent risk taking. To make entrepreneurship easier, they discouraged unnecessary bureaucracy. They also upgraded hiring standards and created the TRS Graduate Management Program, which offered high-potential young people special training, an enriched set of experiences, and an unusual degree of exposure to people in top management. To encourage risk taking among all TRS employees, Gerstner also established something called the Great Performers program to recognize and reward truly exceptional customer service, a central tenet in the organization's vision.

These incentives led quickly to new markets, products, and services. TRS expanded its overseas presence dramatically. By 1988, AmEx cards were issued in 29 currencies (as opposed to only 11 a decade earlier). The unit also focused aggressively on two market segments that had historically received little attention: college students and women. In 1981, TRS combined its card and travel-service capabilities to offer corporate clients a unified system to monitor and control travel expenses. And by 1988, AmEx had grown to become the fifth largest direct-mail merchant in the United States.

Other new products and services included 90-day insurance on all purchases made with the AmEx card, a Platinum American Express card, and a revolving credit card known as Optima. In 1988, the company also switched to image-processing technology for billing, producing a more convenient monthly statement for customers and reducing billing costs by 25%.

As a result of these innovations, TRS's net income increased a phenomenal 500% between 1978 and 1987—a compounded annual rate of about 18%. The business outperformed many so-called high-tech/high-growth companies. With a 1988 return on equity of 28%, it also outperformed most low-growth but high-profit businesses.

when organizations attempt to change. Unless many individuals line up and move together in the same direction, people will tend to fall all over one another. To executives who are overeducated in management and undereducated in leadership, the idea of getting people moving in the same direction appears to be an organizational problem. What executives need to do, however, is not organize people but align them.

Managers "organize" to create human systems that can implement plans as precisely and efficiently as possible. Typically, this requires a number of potentially complex decisions. A company must choose a structure of jobs and reporting relationships, staff it with individuals suited to the jobs, provide training for those who need it, communicate plans to the workforce, and decide how much authority to delegate and to whom. Economic incentives also need to be constructed to accomplish the plan, as well as systems to monitor its implementation. These organizational judgments are much like architectural decisions. It's a question of fit within a particular context.

Aligning is different. It is more of a communications challenge than a design problem. Aligning invariably involves talking to many more individuals than organizing does. The target population can involve not only a manager's subordinates but also bosses, peers, staff in other parts of the organization, as well as suppliers, government officials, and even customers. Anyone who can help implement the vision and strategies or who can block implementation is relevant.

Trying to get people to comprehend a vision of an alternative future is also a communications challenge of a completely different magnitude from organizing them to fulfill a short-term plan. It's much like the difference between a football quarterback attempting to describe to his team the next two or three plays versus his trying to explain to them a totally new approach to the game to be used in the second half of the season.

Whether delivered with many words or a few carefully chosen symbols, such messages are not necessarily accepted just because they are understood. Another big challenge in leadership efforts is credibility—getting people to believe the message. Many things contribute to credibility: the track record of the person delivering the message, the content of the message itself, the communicator's reputation for integrity and trustworthiness, and the consistency between words and deeds.

Finally, aligning leads to empowerment in a way that organizing rarely does. One of the reasons some organizations have difficulty adjusting to rapid changes in markets or technology is that so many people in those companies feel relatively powerless. They have learned from experience that even if they correctly perceive important external changes and then initiate appropriate actions, they are vulnerable to someone higher up who does not like what they have done. Reprimands can take many different forms: "That's against policy," or "We can't afford it," or "Shut up and do as you're told."

Alignment helps overcome this problem by empowering people in at least two ways. First, when a clear sense of direction has been communicated throughout an organization, lower-level employees can initiate actions without the same degree of vulnerability. As long as their behavior is consistent with the vision, superiors will have more difficulty reprimanding them. Second, because everyone is aiming at the same target, the probability is less that one person's initiative will be stalled when it comes into conflict with someone else's.

Motivating People Versus Controlling and Problem Solving

Since change is the function of leadership, being able to generate highly energized behavior is important for coping with the inevitable barriers to change. Just as direction setting identifies an appropriate path for movement and just as effective alignment gets people moving down that path, successful motivation ensures that they will have the energy to overcome obstacles.

According to the logic of management, control mechanisms compare system behavior with the plan and take action when a deviation is detected. In a well-managed factory, for example, this means the planning process establishes sensible quality targets, the organizing process builds an organization that can achieve those targets, and a control process makes sure that quality lapses are spotted immediately, not in 30 or 60 days, and corrected.

Motivating People: Richard Nicolosi at Procter & Gamble

FOR ABOUT 20 YEARS AFTER ITS FOUNDING in 1956, Procter & Gamble's paper products division had experienced little competition for its high-quality, reasonably priced, and well-marketed consumer goods. By the late 1970s, however, the market position of the division had changed. New competitive thrusts hurt P&G badly. For example, industry analysts estimate that the company's market share for disposable diapers fell from 75% in the mid-1970s to 52% in 1984.

That year, Richard Nicolosi came to paper products as the associate general manager, after three years in P&G's smaller and faster moving soft-drink business. He found a heavily bureaucratic and centralized organization that was overly preoccupied with internal functional goals and projects. Almost all information about customers came through highly quantitative market research. The technical people were rewarded for cost savings, the commercial people focused on volume and share, and the two groups were nearly at war with each other.

During the late summer of 1984, top management announced that Nicolosi would become the head of paper products in October, and by August he was unofficially running the division. Immediately he began to stress the need for the division to become more creative and market driven, instead of just trying to be a low-cost producer. "I had to make it very clear," Nicolosi later reported, "that the rules of the game had changed."

The new direction included a much greater stress on teamwork and multiple leadership roles. Nicolosi pushed a strategy of using groups to manage the division and its specific products. In October, he and his team designated themselves as the paper division "board" and began meeting first monthly and then weekly. In November, they established "category teams" to manage their major brand groups (like diapers, tissues, towels) and started pushing responsibility down to these teams. "Shun the incremental," Nicolosi stressed, "and go for the leap."

In December, Nicolosi selectively involved himself in more detail in certain activities. He met with the advertising agency and got to know key creative people. He asked the marketing manager of diapers to report directly to him, eliminating a layer in the hierarchy. He talked more to the people who were working on new product development projects.

In January 1985, the board announced a new organizational structure that included not only category teams but also new-brand business teams. By the spring, the board was ready to plan an important motivational event to communicate the new paper products vision to as many people as possible. On June 4, 1985, all the Cincinnati-based personnel in paper plus sales district managers and paper plant managers—several thousand people in all—met in the local Masonic Temple. Nicolosi and other board members described their vision of an organization where "each of us is a leader." The event was videotaped, and an edited version was sent to all sales offices and plants for everyone to see.

All these activities helped create an entrepreneurial environment where large numbers of people were motivated to realize the new vision. Most innovations came from people dealing with new products. Ultra Pampers, first introduced in February 1985, took the market share of the entire Pampers product line from 40% to 58% and profitability from break-even to positive. And within only a few months of the introduction of Luvs Delux in May 1987, market share for the overall brand grew by 150%.

Other employee initiatives were oriented more toward a functional area, and some came from the bottom of the hierarchy. In the spring of 1986, a few of the division's secretaries, feeling empowered by the new culture, developed a secretaries network. This association established subcommittees on training, on rewards and recognition, and on the "secretary of the future." Echoing the sentiments of many of her peers, one paper products secretary said: "I don't see why we, too, can't contribute to the division's new direction."

By the end of 1988, revenues at the paper products division were up 40% over a four-year period. Profits were up 68%. And this happened despite the fact that the competition continued to get tougher.

For some of the same reasons that control is so central to management, highly motivated or inspired behavior is almost irrelevant. Managerial processes must be as close as possible to fail-safe and risk free. That means they cannot be dependent on the unusual or hard to obtain. The whole purpose of systems and structures is to help normal people who behave in normal ways to complete routine jobs successfully, day after day. It's not exciting or glamorous. But that's management.

Leadership is different. Achieving grand visions always requires a burst of energy. Motivation and inspiration energize people, not by pushing them in the right direction as control mechanisms do but by satisfying basic human needs for achievement, a sense of belonging, recognition, self-esteem, a feeling of control over one's life, and the ability to live up to one's ideals. Such feelings touch us deeply and elicit a powerful response.

Good leaders motivate people in a variety of ways. First, they always articulate the organization's vision in a manner that stresses the values of the audience they are addressing. This makes the work important to those individuals. Leaders also regularly involve people in deciding how to achieve the organization's vision (or the part most relevant to a particular individual). This gives people a sense of control. Another important motivational technique is to support employee efforts to realize the vision by providing coaching, feedback, and role modeling, thereby helping people grow professionally and enhancing their self-esteem. Finally, good leaders recognize and reward success, which not only gives people a sense of accomplishment but also makes them feel like they belong to an organization that cares about them. When all this is done, the work itself becomes intrinsically motivating.

The more that change characterizes the business environment, the more that leaders must motivate people to provide leadership as well. When this works, it tends to reproduce leadership across the entire organization, with people occupying multiple leadership roles throughout the hierarchy. This is highly valuable, because coping with change in any complex business demands initiatives from a multitude of people. Nothing less will work.

Of course, leadership from many sources does not necessarily converge. To the contrary, it can easily conflict. For multiple leadership roles to work together, people's actions must be carefully coordinated by mechanisms that differ from those coordinating traditional management roles.

Strong networks of informal relationships—the kind found in companies with healthy cultures—help coordinate leadership activities in much the same way that formal structure coordinates managerial activities. The key difference is that informal networks can deal with the greater demands for coordination associated with nonroutine activities and change. The multitude of communication channels and the trust among the individuals connected by those channels allow for an ongoing process of accommodation and adaptation. When conflicts arise among roles, those same relationships help resolve the conflicts. Perhaps most important, this process of dialogue and accommodation can produce visions that are linked and compatible instead of remote and competitive. All this requires a great deal more communication than is needed to coordinate managerial roles, but unlike formal structure, strong informal networks can handle it.

Informal relations of some sort exist in all corporations. But too often these networks are either very weak—some people are well connected but most are not—or they are highly fragmented—a strong network exists inside the marketing group and inside R&D but not across the two departments. Such networks do not support multiple leadership initiatives well. In fact, extensive informal networks are so important that if they do not exist, creating them has to be the focus of activity early in a major leadership initiative.

Creating a Culture of Leadership

Despite the increasing importance of leadership to business success, the on-the-job experiences of most people actually seem to undermine the development of the attributes needed for leadership. Nevertheless, some companies have consistently demonstrated an ability to develop people into outstanding leader-managers.

Recruiting people with leadership potential is only the first step. Equally important is managing their career patterns. Individuals who are effective in large leadership roles often share a number of career experiences.

Perhaps the most typical and most important is significant challenge early in a career. Leaders almost always have had opportunities during their twenties and thirties to actually try to lead, to take a risk, and to learn from both triumphs and failures. Such learning seems essential in developing a wide range of leadership skills and perspectives. These opportunities also teach people something about both the difficulty of leadership and its potential for producing change.

Later in their careers, something equally important happens that has to do with broadening. People who provide effective leadership in important jobs always have a chance, before they get into those jobs, to grow beyond the narrow base that characterizes most managerial careers. This is usually the result of lateral career moves or of early promotions to unusually broad job assignments. Sometimes other vehicles help, like special task-force assignments or a lengthy general management course. Whatever the case, the breadth of knowledge developed in this way seems to be helpful in all aspects of leadership. So does the network of relationships that is often acquired both inside and outside the company. When enough people get opportunities like this, the relationships that are built also help create the strong informal networks needed to support multiple leadership initiatives.

Corporations that do a better-than-average job of developing leaders put an emphasis on creating challenging opportunities for relatively young employees. In many businesses, decentralization is the key. By definition, it pushes responsibility lower in an organization and in the process creates more challenging jobs at lower levels. Johnson & Johnson, 3M, Hewlett-Packard, General Electric, and many other well-known companies have used that approach quite successfully. Some of those same companies also create as many small units as possible so there are a lot of challenging lower-level general management jobs available.

Sometimes these businesses develop additional challenging opportunities by stressing growth through new products or services. Over the years, 3M has had a policy that at least 25% of its revenue should come from products introduced within the last five years. That encourages small new ventures, which in turn offer hundreds of opportunities to test and stretch young people with leadership potential.

Such practices can, almost by themselves, prepare people for small- and medium-sized leadership jobs. But developing people for important leadership positions requires more work on the part of senior executives, often over a long period of time. That work begins with efforts to spot people with great leadership potential early in their careers and to identify what will be needed to stretch and develop them.

Again, there is nothing magic about this process. The methods successful companies use are surprisingly straightforward. They go out of their way to make young employees and people at lower levels in their organizations visible to senior management. Senior managers then judge for themselves who has potential and what the development needs of those people are. Executives also discuss their tentative conclusions among themselves to draw more accurate judgments.

Armed with a clear sense of who has considerable leadership potential and what skills they need to develop, executives in these companies then spend time planning for that development. Sometimes that is done as part of a formal succession planning or high-potential development process; often it is more informal. In either case, the key ingredient appears to be an intelligent assessment of what feasible development opportunities fit each candidate's needs.

To encourage managers to participate in these activities, well-led businesses tend to recognize and reward people who successfully develop leaders. This is rarely done as part of a formal compensation or bonus formula, simply because it is so difficult to measure such achievements with precision. But it does become a factor in decisions about promotion, especially to the most senior levels, and that seems to make a big difference. When told that future promotions will depend to some degree on their ability to nurture leaders, even people who say that leadership cannot be developed somehow find ways to do it.

Such strategies help create a corporate culture where people value strong leadership and strive to create it. Just as we need more people to provide leadership in the complex organizations that dominate our world today, we also need more people to develop the cultures that will create that leadership. Institutionalizing a leadership-centered culture is the ultimate act of leadership.

Originally published in May 1990. Reprint R0111F

Level 5 Leadership

The Triumph of Humility and
Fierce Resolve. *by Jim Collins*

IN 1971, A SEEMINGLY ordinary man named Darwin E. Smith was named chief executive of Kimberly-Clark, a stodgy old paper company whose stock had fallen 36% behind the general market during the previous 20 years. Smith, the company's mild-mannered in-house lawyer, wasn't so sure the board had made the right choice—a feeling that was reinforced when a Kimberly-Clark director pulled him aside and reminded him that he lacked some of the qualifications for the position. But CEO he was, and CEO he remained for 20 years.

What a 20 years it was. In that period, Smith created a stunning transformation at Kimberly-Clark, turning it into the leading consumer paper products company in the world. Under his stewardship, the company beat its rivals Scott Paper and Procter & Gamble. And in doing so, Kimberly-Clark generated cumulative stock returns that were 4.1 times greater than those of the general market, outperforming venerable companies such as Hewlett-Packard, 3M, Coca-Cola, and General Electric.

Smith's turnaround of Kimberly-Clark is one the best examples in the twentieth century of a leader taking a company from merely good to truly great. And yet few people—even ardent students of business history—have heard of Darwin Smith. He probably would have liked it that way. Smith is a classic example of a Level 5 leader—an individual who blends extreme personal humility with intense professional will. According to our five-year research study, executives who possess this paradoxical combination of traits are catalysts for

57

the statistically rare event of transforming a good company into a great one. (The research is described in the sidebar "One Question, Five Years, 11 Companies.")

"Level 5" refers to the highest level in a hierarchy of executive capabilities that we identified during our research. Leaders at the other four levels in the hierarchy can produce high degrees of success but not enough to elevate companies from mediocrity to sustained excellence. (For more details about this concept, see the exhibit "The Level 5 hierarchy.") And while Level 5 leadership is not the only requirement for transforming a good company into a great one—other factors include getting the right people on the bus (and

---

The Level 5 hierarchy

The Level 5 leader sits on top of a hierarchy of capabilities and is, according to our research, a necessary requirement for transforming an organization from good to great. But what lies beneath? Four other layers, each one appropriate in its own right but none with the power of Level 5. Individuals do not need to proceed sequentially through each level of the hierarchy to reach the top, but to be a full-fledged Level 5 requires the capabilities of all the lower levels, plus the special characteristics of Level 5.

Level 5

Executive: Builds enduring greatness through a paradoxical combination of personal humility plus professional will.

Level 4

Effective leader: Catalyzes commitment to and vigorous pursuit of a clear and compelling vision; stimulates the group to high performance standards.

Level 3

Competent manager: Organizes people and resources toward the effective and efficient pursuit of predetermined objectives.

Level 2

Contributing team member: Contributes to the achievement of group objectives; works effectively with others in a group setting.

Level 1

Highly capable individual: Makes productive contributions through talent, knowledge, skills, and good work habits.

Idea in Brief

Out of 1,435 *Fortune* 500 companies that renowned management researcher Jim Collins studied, only 11 achieved and sustained greatness—garnering stock returns at least three times the market's—for 15 years after a major transition period.

What did these 11 companies have in common? Each had a "Level 5" leader at the helm.

Level 5 leaders blend the paradoxical combination of **deep personal humility** with **intense professional will**. This rare combination also defies our assumptions about what makes a great leader.

Celebrities like Lee Iacocca may make headlines. But mild-mannered, steely leaders like Darwin Smith of Kimberly-Clark boost their companies to greatness—and keep them there.

Example: Darwin Smith—CEO at paper-products maker Kimberly-Clark from 1971 to 1991—epitomizes Level 5 leadership. Shy, awkward, shunning attention, he also showed iron will, determinedly redefining the firm's core business despite Wall Street's skepticism. The formerly lackluster Kimberly-Clark became the worldwide leader in its industry, generating stock returns 4.1 times greater than the general market's.

the wrong people off the bus) and creating a culture of discipline—our research shows it to be essential. Good-to-great transformations don't happen without Level 5 leaders at the helm. They just don't.

Not What You Would Expect

Our discovery of Level 5 leadership is counterintuitive. Indeed, it is countercultural. People generally assume that transforming companies from good to great requires larger-than-life leaders—big personalities like Lee Iacocca, Al Dunlap, Jack Welch, and Stanley Gault, who make headlines and become celebrities.

Compared with those CEOs, Darwin Smith seems to have come from Mars. Shy, unpretentious, even awkward, Smith shunned attention. When a journalist asked him to describe his management style, Smith just stared back at the scribe from the other side of his thick black-rimmed glasses. He was dressed unfashionably, like a

Idea in Practice

Humility + Will = Level 5

How do Level 5 leaders manifest humility? They routinely credit others, external factors, and good luck for their companies' success. But when results are poor, they blame themselves. They also act quietly, calmly, and determinedly—relying on inspired standards, not inspiring charisma, to motivate.

Inspired standards demonstrate Level 5 leaders' unwavering will. Utterly intolerant of mediocrity, they are stoic in their resolve to do whatever it takes to produce great results—terminating everything else. And they select

superb successors, wanting their companies to become even more successful in the future.

Can You Develop Level 5 Leadership?

Level 5 leaders sit atop a hierarchy of four more common leadership levels—and possess the skills of all four. For example, Level 4 leaders catalyze commitment to and vigorous pursuit of a clear, compelling vision. Can you move from Level 4 to Level 5? Perhaps, *if* you have the Level 5 "seed" within you.

Leaders *without* the seed tend to have monumental egos they can't subjugate to something larger

farm boy wearing his first J.C. Penney suit. Finally, after a long and uncomfortable silence, he said, "Eccentric." Needless to say, the *Wall Street Journal* did not publish a splashy feature on Darwin Smith.

But if you were to consider Smith soft or meek, you would be terribly mistaken. His lack of pretense was coupled with a fierce, even stoic, resolve toward life. Smith grew up on an Indiana farm and put himself through night school at Indiana University by working the day shift at International Harvester. One day, he lost a finger on the job. The story goes that he went to class that evening and returned to work the very next day. Eventually, this poor but determined Indiana farm boy earned admission to Harvard Law School.

He showed the same iron will when he was at the helm of Kimberly-Clark. Indeed, two months after Smith became CEO, doctors diagnosed him with nose and throat cancer and told him he had less than a year to live. He duly informed the board of his illness but said he had no plans to die anytime soon. Smith held to his demanding work schedule while commuting weekly from Wisconsin and more sustaining than themselves, i.e., their companies. But for leaders *with* the seed, the right conditions—such as self-reflection or a profoundly transformative event, such as a life-threatening illness—can stimulate the seed to sprout.

Growing to Level 5

Grow Level 5 seeds by practicing these good-to-great disciplines of Level 5 leaders.

First Who

Attend to people first, strategy second. Get the right people on the bus and the wrong people off—*then* figure out where to drive it.

Stockdale Paradox

Deal with the brutal facts of your current reality—while maintaining absolute faith that you'll prevail.

Buildup-Breakthrough Flywheel

Keep pushing your organizational "flywheel." With consistent effort, momentum increases until—bang!—the wheel hits the breakthrough point.

The Hedgehog Concept

Think of your company as three intersecting circles: what it can be best at, how its economics work best, and what ignites its people's passions. Eliminate *everything* else.

to Houston for radiation therapy. He lived 25 more years, 20 of them as CEO.

Smith's ferocious resolve was crucial to the rebuilding of Kimberly-Clark, especially when he made the most dramatic decision in the company's history: selling the mills.

To explain: Shortly after he took over, Smith and his team had concluded that the company's traditional core business—coated paper—was doomed to mediocrity. Its economics were bad and the competition weak. But, they reasoned, if Kimberly-Clark were thrust into the fire of the consumer paper products business, better economics and world-class competition like Procter & Gamble would force it to achieve greatness or perish.

And so, like the general who burned the boats upon landing on enemy soil, leaving his troops to succeed or die, Smith announced that Kimberly-Clark would sell its mills—even the namesake mill in Kimberly, Wisconsin. All proceeds would be thrown into the consumer business, with investments in brands like Huggies diapers

One Question, Five Years, 11 Companies

THE LEVEL 5 DISCOVERY DERIVES from a research project that began in 1996, when my research teams and I set out to answer one question: Can a good company become a great company and, if so, how? Most great companies grew up with superb parents—people like George Merck, David Packard, and Walt Disney—who instilled greatness early on. But what about the vast majority of companies that wake up partway through life and realize that they're good but not great?

To answer that question, we looked for companies that had shifted from good performance to great performance—and sustained it. We identified comparison companies that had failed to make that sustained shift. We then studied the contrast between the two groups to discover common variables that distinguished those who made and sustained a shift from those who could have but didn't.

More precisely, we searched for a specific pattern: cumulative stock returns at or below the general stock market for 15 years, punctuated by a transition point, then cumulative returns at least three times the market over the next 15 years. (See the accompanying exhibit.) We used data from the University of Chicago Center for Research in Security Prices and adjusted for stock splits and all dividends reinvested. The shift had to be distinct from the industry; if the whole industry showed the same shift, we'd drop the company. We began with 1,435 companies that appeared on the *Fortune* 500 from 1965 to 1995; we found 11 good-to-great examples. That's not a sample; that's the total number that jumped all our hurdles and passed into the study.

Those that made the cut averaged cumulative stock returns 6.9 times the general stock market for the 15 years after the point of transition. To put that in perspective, General Electric under Jack Welch outperformed the general stock market by 2.8:1 during his tenure from 1986 to 2000. One dollar invested in a mutual fund of the good-to-great companies in 1965 grew to $470 by 2000 compared with $56 in the general stock market. These are remarkable numbers, made all the more so by the fact that they came from previously unremarkable companies.

For each good-to-great example, we selected the best direct comparison, based on similarity of business, size, age, customers, and performance leading up to the transition. We also constructed a set of six "unsustained" comparisons (companies that showed a short-lived shift but then fell off) to address the question of sustainability. To be conservative, we consistently picked comparison companies that, if anything, were in better shape than the good-to-great companies were in the years just before the transition.

With 22 research associates working in groups of four to six at a time from 1996 to 2000, our study involved a wide range of both qualitative and quantitative analyses. On the qualitative front, we collected nearly 6,000 articles, conducted 87 interviews with key executives, analyzed companies' internal strategy documents, and culled through analysts' reports. On the quantitative front, we ran financial metrics, examined executive compensation, compared patterns of management turnover, quantified company layoffs and restructurings, and calculated the effect of acquisitions and divestitures on companies' stocks. We then synthesized the results to identify the drivers of good-to-great transformations. One was Level 5 leadership. (The others are described in the sidebar "Not by Level 5 Alone.")

Since only 11 companies qualified as good-to-great, a research finding had to meet a stiff standard before we would deem it significant. Every component in the final framework showed up in all 11 good-to-great companies during the transition era, regardless of industry (from steel to banking), transition decade (from the 1950s to the 1990s), circumstances (from plodding along to dire crisis), or size (from tens of millions to tens of billions). Additionally, every component had to show up in less than 30% of the comparison companies during the relevant years. Level 5 easily made it into the framework as one of the strongest, most consistent contrasts between the good-to-great and the comparison companies.

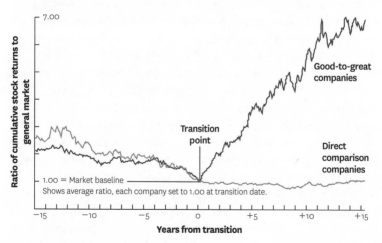

63

and Kleenex tissues. The business media called the move stupid, and Wall Street analysts downgraded the stock. But Smith never wavered. Twenty-five years later, Kimberly-Clark owned Scott Paper and beat Procter & Gamble in six of eight product categories. In retirement, Smith reflected on his exceptional performance, saying simply, "I never stopped trying to become qualified for the job."

Not What We Expected, Either

We'll look in depth at Level 5 leadership, but first let's set an important context for our findings. We were not looking for Level 5 or anything like it. Our original question was, Can a good company become a great one and, if so, how? In fact, I gave the research teams explicit instructions to downplay the role of top executives in their analyses of this question so we wouldn't slip into the simplistic "credit the leader" or "blame the leader" thinking that is so common today.

But Level 5 found us. Over the course of the study, research teams kept saying, "We can't ignore the top executives even if we want to. There is something consistently unusual about them." I would push back, arguing, "The comparison companies also had leaders. So what's different here?" Back and forth the debate raged. Finally, as should always be the case, the data won. The executives at companies that went from good to great and sustained that performance for 15 years or more were all cut from the same cloth—one remarkably different from that which produced the executives at the comparison companies in our study. It didn't matter whether the company was in crisis or steady state, consumer or industrial, offering services or products. It didn't matter when the transition took place or how big the company. The successful organizations all had a Level 5 leader at the time of transition.

Furthermore, the absence of Level 5 leadership showed up consistently across the comparison companies. The point: Level 5 is an empirical finding, not an ideological one. And that's important to note, given how much the Level 5 finding contradicts not only conventional wisdom but much of management theory to date. (For more about our findings on good-to-great transformations, see the sidebar "Not by Level 5 Alone.")

Humility + Will = Level 5

Level 5 leaders are a study in duality: modest and willful, shy and fearless. To grasp this concept, consider Abraham Lincoln, who never let his ego get in the way of his ambition to create an enduring great nation. Author Henry Adams called him "a quiet, peaceful, shy figure." But those who thought Lincoln's understated manner signaled weakness in the man found themselves terribly mistaken—to the scale of 250,000 Confederate and 360,000 Union lives, including Lincoln's own.

It might be a stretch to compare the 11 Level 5 CEOs in our research to Lincoln, but they did display the same kind of duality. Take Colman M. Mockler, CEO of Gillette from 1975 to 1991. Mockler, who faced down three takeover attempts, was a reserved, gracious man with a gentle, almost patrician manner. Despite epic battles with raiders—he took on Ronald Perelman twice and the former Coniston Partners once—he never lost his shy, courteous style. At the height of crisis, he maintained a calm business-as-usual demeanor, dispensing first with ongoing business before turning to the takeover.

And yet, those who mistook Mockler's outward modesty as a sign of inner weakness were beaten in the end. In one proxy battle, Mockler and other senior executives called thousands of investors, one by one, to win their votes. Mockler simply would not give in. He chose to fight for the future greatness of Gillette even though he could have pocketed millions by flipping his stock.

Consider the consequences had Mockler capitulated. If a share flipper had accepted the full 44% price premium offered by Perelman and then invested those shares in the general market for ten years, he still would have come out 64% behind a shareholder who stayed with Mockler and Gillette. If Mockler had given up the fight, it's likely that none of us would be shaving with Sensor, Lady Sensor, or the Mach III—and hundreds of millions of people would have a more painful battle with daily stubble.

Sadly, Mockler never had the chance to enjoy the full fruits of his efforts. In January 1991, Gillette received an advance copy of *Forbes*.

Not by Level 5 Alone

LEVEL 5 LEADERSHIP is an essential factor for taking a company from good to great, but it's not the only one. Our research uncovered multiple factors that deliver companies to greatness. And it is the combined package—Level 5 plus these other drivers—that takes companies beyond unremarkable. There is a symbiotic relationship between Level 5 and the rest of our findings: Level 5 enables implementation of the other findings, and practicing the other findings may help you get to Level 5. We've already talked about who Level 5 leaders are; the rest of our findings describe what they do. Here is a brief look at some of the other key findings.

First Who

We expected that good-to-great leaders would start with the vision and strategy. Instead, they attended to people first, strategy second. They got the right people on the bus, moved the wrong people off, ushered the right people to the right seats—and then they figured out where to drive it.

Stockdale Paradox

This finding is named after Admiral James Stockdale, winner of the Medal of Honor, who survived seven years in a Vietcong POW camp by hanging on to two contradictory beliefs: His life couldn't be worse at the moment, and his life would someday be better than ever. Like Stockdale, people at the good-to-great companies in our research confronted the most brutal facts of their current reality, yet simultaneously maintained absolute faith that they would prevail in the end. And they held both disciplines—faith and facts—at the same time, all the time.

Buildup-Breakthrough Flywheel

Good-to-great transformations do not happen overnight or in one big leap. Rather, the process resembles relentlessly pushing a giant, heavy flywheel in one direction. At first, pushing it gets the flywheel to turn once. With consistent effort, it goes two turns, then five, then ten, building increasing momentum until—bang!—the wheel hits the breakthrough point, and the momentum

---

The cover featured an artist's rendition of the publicity-shy Mockler standing on a mountaintop, holding a giant razor above his head in a triumphant pose. Walking back to his office just minutes after seeing this public acknowledgment of his 16 years of struggle, Mockler crumpled to the floor and died of a massive heart attack.

really kicks in. Our comparison companies never sustained the kind of breakthrough momentum that the good-to-great companies did; instead, they lurched back and forth with radical change programs, reactionary moves, and restructurings.

The Hedgehog Concept

In a famous essay, philosopher and scholar Isaiah Berlin described two approaches to thought and life using a simple parable: The fox knows a little about many things, but the hedgehog knows only one big thing very well. The fox is complex; the hedgehog simple. And the hedgehog wins. Our research shows that breakthroughs require a simple, hedgehog-like understanding of three intersecting circles: what a company can be the best in the world at, how its economics work best, and what best ignites the passions of its people. Breakthroughs happen when you get the hedgehog concept and become systematic and consistent with it, eliminating virtually anything that does not fit in the three circles.

Technology Accelerators

The good-to-great companies had a paradoxical relationship with technology. On the one hand, they assiduously avoided jumping on new technology bandwagons. On the other, they were pioneers in the application of carefully selected technologies, making bold, farsighted investments in those that directly linked to their hedgehog concept. Like turbochargers, these technology accelerators create an explosion in flywheel momentum.

A Culture of Discipline

When you look across the good-to-great transformations, they consistently display three forms of discipline: disciplined people, disciplined thought, and disciplined action. When you have disciplined people, you don't need hierarchy. When you have disciplined thought, you don't need bureaucracy. When you have disciplined action, you don't need excessive controls. When you combine a culture of discipline with an ethic of entrepreneurship, you get the magical alchemy of great performance.

Even if Mockler had known he would die in office, he could not have changed his approach. His placid persona hid an inner intensity, a dedication to making anything he touched the best—not just because of what he would get but because he couldn't imagine doing it any other way. Mockler could not give up the company to those who would destroy it, any more than Lincoln would risk losing the chance to build an enduring great nation.

A Compelling Modesty

The Mockler story illustrates the modesty typical of Level 5 leaders. (For a summary of Level 5 traits, see the exhibit "The Yin and Yang of Level 5.") Indeed, throughout our interviews with such executives, we were struck by the way they talked about themselves—or rather, didn't talk about themselves. They'd go on and on about the company and the contributions of other executives, but they would instinctively deflect discussion about their own role. When pressed to talk about themselves, they'd say things like, "I hope I'm not sounding like a big shot," or "I don't think I can take much credit for what happened. We were blessed with marvelous people." One Level 5 leader even asserted, "There are a lot of people in this company who could do my job better than I do."

By contrast, consider the courtship of personal celebrity by the comparison CEOs. Scott Paper, the comparison company to Kimberly-Clark, hired Al Dunlap as CEO—a man who would tell anyone who would listen (and many who would have preferred not to) about his accomplishments. After 19 months atop Scott Paper, Dunlap said in *BusinessWeek,* "The Scott story will go down in the annals of American business history as one of the most successful, quickest turnarounds ever. It makes other turnarounds pale by comparison." He personally accrued $100 million for 603 days of work at Scott Paper—about $165,000 per day—largely by slashing the workforce, halving the R&D budget, and putting the company on growth steroids in preparation for sale. After selling off the company and pocketing his quick millions, Dunlap wrote an autobiography in which he boastfully dubbed himself "Rambo in pinstripes." It's hard to imagine Darwin Smith thinking, "Hey, that Rambo character reminds me of me," let alone stating it publicly.

Granted, the Scott Paper story is one of the more dramatic in our study, but it's not an isolated case. In more than two-thirds of the comparison companies, we noted the presence of a gargantuan ego

The Yin and Yang of Level 5

Personal humility

Demonstrates a compelling modesty, shunning public adulation; never boastful.

Acts with quiet, calm determination; relies principally on inspired standards, not inspiring charisma, to motivate.

Channels ambition into the company, not the self; sets up successors for even more greatness in the next generation.

Looks in the mirror, not out the window, to apportion responsibility for poor results, never blaming other people, external factors, or bad luck.

Professional will

Creates superb results, a clear catalyst in the transition from good to great.

Demonstrates an unwavering resolve to do whatever must be done to produce the best long-term results, no matter how difficult.

Sets the standard of building an enduring, great company; will settle for nothing less.

Looks out the window, not in the mirror, to apportion credit for the success of the company—to other people, external factors, and good luck.

---

that contributed to the demise or continued mediocrity of the company. We found this pattern particularly strong in the unsustained comparison companies—the companies that would show a shift in performance under a talented yet egocentric Level 4 leader, only to decline in later years.

Lee Iacocca, for example, saved Chrysler from the brink of catastrophe, performing one of the most celebrated (and deservedly so) turnarounds in U.S. business history. The automaker's stock rose 2.9 times higher than the general market about halfway through his tenure. But then Iacocca diverted his attention to transforming himself. He appeared regularly on talk shows like the *Today Show* and *Larry King Live,* starred in more than 80 commercials, entertained the idea of running for president of the United States, and promoted his autobiography, which sold 7 million copies worldwide. Iacocca's personal stock soared, but Chrysler's stock fell 31% below the market in the second half of his tenure.

And once Iacocca had accumulated all the fame and perks, he found it difficult to leave center stage. He postponed his retirement so many times that Chrysler's insiders began to joke that Iacocca stood for "I Am Chairman of Chrysler Corporation Always." When he finally retired, he demanded that the board continue to provide a private jet and stock options. Later, he joined forces with noted takeover artist Kirk Kerkorian to launch a hostile bid for Chrysler. (It failed.) Iacocca did make one final brilliant decision: He picked a modest yet determined man—perhaps even a Level 5—as his successor. Bob Eaton rescued Chrysler from its second near-death crisis in a decade and set the foundation for a more enduring corporate transition.

An Unwavering Resolve

Besides extreme humility, Level 5 leaders also display tremendous professional will. When George Cain became CEO of Abbott Laboratories, it was a drowsy, family-controlled business sitting at the bottom quartile of the pharmaceutical industry, living off its cash cow, erythromycin. Cain was a typical Level 5 leader in his lack of pretense; he didn't have the kind of inspiring personality that would galvanize the company. But he had something much more powerful: inspired standards. He could not stand mediocrity in any form and was utterly intolerant of anyone who would accept the idea that good is good enough. For the next 14 years, he relentlessly imposed his will for greatness on Abbott Labs.

Among Cain's first tasks was to destroy one of the root causes of Abbott's middling performance: nepotism. By systematically rebuilding both the board and the executive team with the best people he could find, Cain made his statement. Family ties no longer mattered. If you couldn't become the best executive in the industry within your span of responsibility, you would lose your paycheck.

Such near-ruthless rebuilding might be expected from an outsider brought in to turn the company around, but Cain was an 18-year insider—and a part of the family, the son of a previous president. Holiday gatherings were probably tense for a few years in the Cain clan—"Sorry I had to fire you. Want another slice of turkey?"—but in the end, family members were pleased with the performance of their stock. Cain had set in motion a profitable growth machine. From its transition in 1974 to 2000, Abbott created shareholder returns that beat the market 4.5:1, outperforming industry superstars Merck and Pfizer by a factor of two.

Another good example of iron-willed Level 5 leadership comes from Charles R. "Cork" Walgreen III, who transformed dowdy Walgreens into a company that outperformed the stock market 16:1 from its transition in 1975 to 2000. After years of dialogue and debate within his executive team about what to do with Walgreens' food-service operations, this CEO sensed the team had finally reached a watershed: The company's brightest future lay in convenient drugstores, not in food service. Dan Jorndt, who succeeded Walgreen in 1988, describes what happened next:

> Cork said at one of our planning committee meetings, "Okay, now I am going to draw the line in the sand. We are going to be out of the restaurant business completely in five years." At the time we had more than 500 restaurants. You could have heard a pin drop. He said, "I want to let everybody know the clock is ticking." Six months later we were at our next planning committee meeting and someone mentioned just in passing that we had only five years to be out of the restaurant business. Cork was not a real vociferous fellow. He sort of tapped on the table and said, "Listen, you now have four-and-a-half years. I said you had five years six months ago. Now you've got four-and-a-half years." Well, that next day things really clicked into gear for winding down our restaurant business. Cork never wavered. He never doubted. He never second-guessed.

Like Darwin Smith selling the mills at Kimberly-Clark, Cork Walgreen required stoic resolve to make his decisions. Food service was not the largest part of the business, although it did add substantial profits to the bottom line. The real problem was more emotional than financial. Walgreens had, after all, invented the malted milk shake, and food service had been a long-standing family tradition dating back to Cork's grandfather. Not only that, some food-service outlets were even named after the CEO—for example, a restaurant chain named Corky's. But no matter; if Walgreen had to fly in the face of family tradition in order to refocus on the one arena in which Walgreens could be the best in the world—convenient drugstores—and terminate everything else that would not produce great results, then Cork would do it. Quietly, doggedly, simply.

One final, yet compelling, note on our findings about Level 5: Because Level 5 leaders have ambition not for themselves but for their companies, they routinely select superb successors. Level 5 leaders want to see their companies become even more successful in the next generation and are comfortable with the idea that most people won't even know that the roots of that success trace back to them. As one Level 5 CEO said, "I want to look from my porch, see the company as one of the great companies in the world someday, and be able to say, 'I used to work there.'" By contrast, Level 4 leaders often fail to set up the company for enduring success. After all, what better testament to your own personal greatness than that the place falls apart after you leave?

In more than three-quarters of the comparison companies, we found executives who set up their successors for failure, chose weak successors, or both. Consider the case of Rubbermaid, which grew from obscurity to become one of *Fortune*'s most admired companies—and then, just as quickly, disintegrated into such sorry shape that it had to be acquired by Newell.

The architect of this remarkable story was a charismatic and brilliant leader named Stanley C. Gault, whose name became synonymous in the late 1980s with Rubbermaid's success. Across the 312 articles collected by our research team about the company, Gault comes through as a hard-driving, egocentric executive. In one article, he responds to the accusation of being a tyrant with the statement, "Yes, but I'm a sincere tyrant." In another, drawn directly from his own comments on leading change, the word "I" appears 44 times, while the word "we" appears 16 times. Of course, Gault had every reason to be proud of his executive success: Rubbermaid generated 40 consecutive quarters of earnings growth under his leadership—an impressive performance, to be sure, and one that deserves respect.

But Gault did not leave behind a company that would be great without him. His chosen successor lasted a year on the job and the next in line faced a management team so shallow that he had to temporarily shoulder four jobs while scrambling to identify a new number-two executive. Gault's successors struggled not only with a management void but also with strategic voids that would eventually bring the company to its knees.

Of course, you might say—as one *Fortune* article did—that the fact that Rubbermaid fell apart after Gault left proves his greatness as a leader. Gault was a tremendous Level 4 leader, perhaps one of the best in the last 50 years. But he was not at Level 5, and that is one crucial reason why Rubbermaid went from good to great for a brief, shining moment and then just as quickly went from great to irrelevant.

The Window and the Mirror

As part of our research, we interviewed Alan L. Wurtzel, the Level 5 leader responsible for turning Circuit City from a ramshackle company on the edge of bankruptcy into one of America's most successful electronics retailers. In the 15 years after its transition date in 1982, Circuit City outperformed the market 18.5:1.

We asked Wurtzel to list the top five factors in his company's transformation, ranked by importance. His number one factor? Luck. "We were in a great industry, with the wind at our backs," he said. But wait a minute, we retorted, Silo—your comparison company—was in the same industry, with the same wind and bigger sails. The conversation went back and forth, with Wurtzel refusing to take much credit for the transition, preferring to attribute it largely to just being in the right place at the right time. Later, when we asked him to discuss the factors that would sustain a good-to-great transformation, he said, "The first thing that comes to mind is luck. I was lucky to find the right successor."

Luck. What an odd factor to talk about. Yet the Level 5 leaders we identified invoked it frequently. We asked an executive at steel company Nucor why it had such a remarkable track record for making good decisions. His response? "I guess we were just lucky." Joseph F. Cullman III, the Level 5 CEO of Philip Morris, flat out refused to take credit for his company's success, citing his good fortune to have great colleagues, successors, and predecessors. Even the book he wrote about his career—which he penned at the urging of his colleagues and which he never intended to distribute widely outside the company—had the unusual title *I'm a Lucky Guy*.

At first, we were puzzled by the Level 5 leaders' emphasis on good luck. After all, there is no evidence that the companies that had progressed from good to great were blessed with more good luck (or more bad luck, for that matter) than the comparison companies. But then we began to notice an interesting pattern in the executives at the comparison companies: They often blamed their situations on bad luck, bemoaning the difficulties of the environment they faced.

Compare Bethlehem Steel and Nucor, for example. Both steel companies operated with products that are hard to differentiate, and both faced a competitive challenge from cheap imported steel. Both companies paid significantly higher wages than most of their foreign competitors. And yet executives at the two companies held completely different views of the same environment.

Bethlehem Steel's CEO summed up the company's problems in 1983 by blaming the imports: "Our first, second, and third problems are imports." Meanwhile, Ken Iverson and his crew at Nucor saw the imports as a blessing: "Aren't we lucky; steel is heavy, and they have to ship it all the way across the ocean, giving us a huge advantage." Indeed, Iverson saw the first, second, and third problems facing the U.S. steel industry not in imports but in management. He even went so far as to speak out publicly against government protection against imports, telling a gathering of stunned steel executives in 1977 that the real problems facing the industry lay in the fact that management had failed to keep pace with technology.

The emphasis on luck turns out to be part of a broader pattern that we have come to call "the window and the mirror." Level 5 leaders, inherently humble, look out the window to apportion credit—even undue credit—to factors outside themselves. If they can't find a specific person or event to give credit to, they credit good luck. At the same time, they look in the mirror to assign responsibility, never citing bad luck or external factors when things go poorly. Conversely, the comparison executives frequently looked out the window for factors to blame but preened in the mirror to credit themselves when things went well.

The funny thing about the window-and-mirror concept is that it does not reflect reality. According to our research, the Level 5 leaders were responsible for their companies' transformations. But they would never admit that. We can't climb inside their heads and assess whether they deeply believed what they saw through the window and in the mirror. But it doesn't really matter, because they acted as if they believed it, and they acted with such consistency that it produced exceptional results.

Born or Bred?

Not long ago, I shared the Level 5 finding with a gathering of senior executives. A woman who had recently become chief executive of her company raised her hand. "I believe what you've told us about Level 5 leadership," she said, "but I'm disturbed because I know I'm not there yet, and maybe I never will be. Part of the reason I got this job is because of my strong ego. Are you telling me that I can't make my company great if I'm not Level 5?"

"Let me return to the data," I responded. "Of 1,435 companies that appeared on the *Fortune* 500 since 1965, only 11 made it into our study. In those 11, all of them had Level 5 leaders in key positions, including the CEO role, at the pivotal time of transition. Now, to reiterate, we're not saying that Level 5 is the only element required for the move from good to great, but it appears to be essential."

She sat there, quiet for a moment, and you could guess what many people in the room were thinking. Finally, she raised her hand again. "Can you learn to become Level 5?" I still do not know the answer to that question. Our research, frankly, did not delve into how Level 5 leaders come to be, nor did we attempt to explain or codify the nature of their emotional lives. We speculated on the unique psychology of Level 5 leaders. Were they "guilty" of displacement—shifting their own raw ambition onto something other than themselves? Were they sublimating their egos for dark and complex reasons rooted in childhood trauma? Who knows? And perhaps more important, do the psychological roots of Level 5 leadership matter any more than do the roots of charisma or intelligence? The question remains: Can Level 5 be developed?

My preliminary hypothesis is that there are two categories of people: those who don't have the Level 5 seed within them and those who do. The first category consists of people who could never in a million years bring themselves to subjugate their own needs to the greater ambition of something larger and more lasting than themselves. For those people, work will always be first and foremost about what they get—the fame, fortune, power, adulation, and so on. Work will never be about what they build, create, and contribute. The great irony is that the animus and personal ambition that often drives people to become a Level 4 leader stands at odds with the humility required to rise to Level 5.

When you combine that irony with the fact that boards of directors frequently operate under the false belief that a larger-than-life, egocentric leader is required to make a company great, you can quickly see why Level 5 leaders rarely appear at the top of our institutions. We keep putting people in positions of power who lack the seed to become a Level 5 leader, and that is one major reason why there are so few companies that make a sustained and verifiable shift from good to great.

The second category consists of people who could evolve to Level 5; the capability resides within them, perhaps buried or ignored or simply nascent. Under the right circumstances—with self-reflection, a mentor, loving parents, a significant life experience, or other factors—the seed can begin to develop. Some of the Level 5 leaders in our study had significant life experiences that might have sparked development of the seed. Darwin Smith fully blossomed as a Level 5 after his near-death experience with cancer. Joe Cullman was profoundly affected by his World War II experiences, particularly the last-minute change of orders that took him off a doomed ship on which he surely would have died; he considered the next 60-odd years a great gift. A strong religious belief or conversion might also nurture the seed. Colman Mockler, for example, converted to evangelical Christianity while getting his MBA at Harvard, and later, according to the book *Cutting Edge* by Gordon McKibben, he became a prime mover in a group of Boston business executives that met frequently over breakfast to discuss the carryover of religious values to corporate life.

We would love to be able to give you a list of steps for getting to Level 5—other than contracting cancer, going through a religious conversion, or getting different parents—but we have no solid research data that would support a credible list. Our research exposed Level 5 as a key component inside the black box of what it takes to shift a company from good to great. Yet inside that black box is another—the inner development of a person to Level 5 leadership. We could speculate on what that inner box might hold, but it would mostly be just that: speculation.

In short, Level 5 is a very satisfying idea, a truthful idea, a powerful idea, and, to make the move from good to great, very likely an essential idea. But to provide "ten steps to Level 5 leadership" would trivialize the concept.

My best advice, based on the research, is to practice the other good-to-great disciplines that we discovered. Since we found a tight symbiotic relationship between each of the other findings and Level 5, we suspect that conscientiously trying to lead using the other disciplines can help you move in the right direction. There is no guarantee that doing so will turn executives into full-fledged Level 5 leaders, but it gives them a tangible place to begin, especially if they have the seed within.

We cannot say for sure what percentage of people have the seed within, nor how many of those can nurture it enough to become Level 5. Even those of us on the research team who identified Level 5 do not know whether we will succeed in evolving to its heights. And yet all of us who worked on the finding have been inspired by the idea of trying to move toward Level 5. Darwin Smith, Colman Mockler, Alan Wurtzel, and all the other Level 5 leaders we learned about have become role models for us. Whether or not we make it to Level 5, it is worth trying. For like all basic truths about what is best in human beings, when we catch a glimpse of that truth, we know that our own lives and all that we touch will be the better for making the effort to get there.

Originally published in January 2001. Reprint R0507M

Reprinted with permission from Jim Collins.

The Work of Leadership

by Ronald A. Heifetz and Donald L. Laurie

TO STAY ALIVE, JACK PRITCHARD had to change his life. Triple bypass surgery and medication could help, the heart surgeon told him, but no technical fix could release Pritchard from his own responsibility for changing the habits of a lifetime. He had to stop smoking, improve his diet, get some exercise, and take time to relax, remembering to breathe more deeply each day. Pritchard's doctor could provide sustaining technical expertise and take supportive action, but only Pritchard could adapt his ingrained habits to improve his long-term health. The doctor faced the leadership task of mobilizing the patient to make critical behavioral changes; Jack Pritchard faced the adaptive work of figuring out which specific changes to make and how to incorporate them into his daily life.

Companies today face challenges similar to the ones that confronted Pritchard and his doctor. They face adaptive challenges. Changes in societies, markets, customers, competition, and technology around the globe are forcing organizations to clarify their values, develop new strategies, and learn new ways of operating. Often the toughest task for leaders in effecting change is mobilizing people throughout the organization to do adaptive work.

Adaptive work is required when our deeply held beliefs are challenged, when the values that made us successful become less relevant, and when legitimate yet competing perspectives emerge. We see adaptive challenges every day at every level of the workplace—when companies restructure or reengineer, develop or implement strategy, or merge businesses. We see adaptive challenges when marketing has difficulty working with operations, when cross-functional teams don't work well, or when senior executives complain, "We don't seem to be able to execute effectively." Adaptive problems are often systemic problems with no ready answers.

Mobilizing an organization to adapt its behaviors in order to thrive in new business environments is critical. Without such change, any company today would falter. Indeed, getting people to do adaptive work is the mark of leadership in a competitive world. Yet for most senior executives, providing leadership and not just authoritative expertise is extremely difficult. Why? We see two reasons. First, in order to make change happen, executives have to break a long-standing behavior pattern of their own: providing leadership in the form of solutions. This tendency is quite natural because many executives reach their positions of authority by virtue of their competence in taking responsibility and solving problems. But the locus of responsibility for problem solving when a company faces an adaptive challenge must shift to its people. Solutions to adaptive challenges reside not in the executive suite but in the collective intelligence of employees at all levels, who need to use one another as resources, often across boundaries, and learn their way to those solutions.

Second, adaptive change is distressing for the people going through it. They need to take on new roles, new relationships, new values, new behaviors, and new approaches to work. Many employees are ambivalent about the efforts and sacrifices required of them. They often look to the senior executive to take problems off their shoulders. But those expectations have to be unlearned. Rather than fulfilling the expectation that they will provide answers, leaders have to ask tough questions. Rather than protecting people from outside threats, leaders should allow them to feel the pinch of reality in order to stimulate them to adapt. Instead of orienting people to their current roles, leaders must disorient them so that new relationships can develop. Instead of quelling conflict, leaders have to

Idea in Brief

What presents your company with its toughest challenges? Shifting markets? Stiffening competition? Emerging technologies? When such challenges intensify, you may need to reclarify corporate values, redesign strategies, merge or dissolve businesses, or manage cross-functional strife.

These **adaptive challenges** are murky, systemic problems with no easy answers. Perhaps even more vexing, the solutions to adaptive challenges *don't* reside in the executive suite. Solving them requires the involvement of people *throughout* your organization.

Adaptive work is tough on everyone. For *leaders*, it's counterintuitive.

Rather than providing solutions, you must ask tough questions and leverage employees' collective intelligence. Instead of maintaining norms, you must challenge the "way we do business." And rather than quelling conflict, you need to draw issues out and let people feel the sting of reality.

For your *employees*, adaptive work is painful—requiring unfamiliar roles, responsibilities, values, and ways of working. No wonder employees often try to lob adaptive work back to their leaders.

How to ensure that you *and* your employees embrace the challenges of adaptive work? Applying the six principles will help.

draw the issues out. Instead of maintaining norms, leaders have to challenge "the way we do business" and help others distinguish immutable values from historical practices that must go.

Drawing on our experience with managers from around the world, we offer six principles for leading adaptive work: "getting on the balcony," identifying the adaptive challenge, regulating distress, maintaining disciplined attention, giving the work back to people, and protecting voices of leadership from below. We illustrate those principles with an example of adaptive change at KPMG Netherlands, a professional-services firm.

Get on the Balcony

Earvin "Magic" Johnson's greatness in leading his basketball team came in part from his ability to play hard while keeping the whole game situation in mind, as if he stood in a press box or on a balcony

Idea in Practice

1. Get on the balcony. Don't get swept up in the field of play. Instead, move back and forth between the "action" and the "balcony." You'll spot emerging patterns, such as power struggles or work avoidance. This high-level perspective helps you mobilize people to do adaptive work.

2. Identify your adaptive challenge.

> *Example:* When British Airways' passengers nicknamed it "Bloody Awful," CEO Colin Marshall knew he had to infuse the company with a dedication to customers. He identified the adaptive challenge as "creating trust throughout British Airways." To diagnose the challenge further, Marshall's team mingled with employees and customers in baggage areas, reservation centers, and planes, asking which beliefs, values, and behaviors needed overhauling. They exposed value-based conflicts underlying surface-level disputes, and resolved the team's own dysfunctional conflicts that impaired companywide collaboration. By understanding themselves, their people, and the company's conflicts, the team strengthened British Airways' bid to become "the World's Favourite Airline."

3. Regulate distress. To inspire change—without disabling people—pace adaptive work:

above the field of play. Bobby Orr played hockey in the same way. Other players might fail to recognize the larger patterns of play that performers like Johnson and Orr quickly understand, because they are so engaged in the game that they get carried away by it. Their attention is captured by the rapid motion, the physical contact, the roar of the crowd, and the pressure to execute. In sports, most players simply may not see who is open for a pass, who is missing a block, or how the offense and defense work together. Players like Johnson and Orr watch these things and allow their observations to guide their actions.

Business leaders have to be able to view patterns as if they were on a balcony. It does them no good to be swept up in the field of action. Leaders have to see a context for change or create one. They should give employees a strong sense of the history of the enterprise

- First, let employees debate issues and clarify assumptions behind competing views—safely.

- Then provide direction. Define *key* issues and values. Control the rate of change: Don't start too many initiatives simultaneously without stopping others.

- Maintain just enough tension, resisting pressure to restore the status quo. Raise tough questions without succumbing to anxiety yourself. Communicate presence and poise.

4. Maintain disciplined attention. Encourage managers to grapple with divisive issues, rather than indulging in scapegoating or denial. Deepen the debate to unlock polarized, superficial conflict. Demonstrate collaboration to solve problems.

5. Give the work back to employees. To instill collective self-confidence—versus dependence on you—support rather than control people. Encourage risk-taking and responsibility—then back people up if they err. Help them recognize they contain the solutions.

6. Protect leadership voices from below. Don't silence whistle-blowers, creative deviants, and others exposing contradictions within your company. Their perspectives can provoke fresh thinking. Ask, "What is this guy *really* talking about? Have we missed something?"

and what's good about its past, as well as an idea of the market forces at work today and the responsibility people must take in shaping the future. Leaders must be able to identify struggles over values and power, recognize patterns of work avoidance, and watch for the many other functional and dysfunctional reactions to change.

Without the capacity to move back and forth between the field of action and the balcony, to reflect day to day, moment to moment, on the many ways in which an organization's habits can sabotage adaptive work, a leader easily and unwittingly becomes a prisoner of the system. The dynamics of adaptive change are far too complex to keep track of, let alone influence, if leaders stay only on the field of play.

We have encountered several leaders, some of whom we discuss in this article, who manage to spend much of their precious time on the balcony as they guide their organizations through change. Without that perspective, they probably would have been unable to mobilize people to do adaptive work. Getting on the balcony is thus a prerequisite for following the next five principles.

Identify the Adaptive Challenge

When a leopard threatens a band of chimpanzees, the leopard rarely succeeds in picking off a stray. Chimps know how to respond to this kind of threat. But when a man with an automatic rifle comes near, the routine responses fail. Chimps risk extinction in a world of poachers unless they figure out how to disarm the new threat. Similarly, when businesses cannot learn quickly to adapt to new challenges, they are likely to face their own form of extinction.

Consider the well-known case of British Airways. Having observed the revolutionary changes in the airline industry during the 1980s, then chief executive Colin Marshall clearly recognized the need to transform an airline nicknamed Bloody Awful by its own passengers into an exemplar of customer service. He also understood that this ambition would require more than anything else changes in values, practices, and relationships throughout the company. An organization whose people clung to functional silos and valued pleasing their bosses more than pleasing customers could not become "the world's favorite airline." Marshall needed an organization dedicated to serving people, acting on trust, respecting the individual, and making teamwork happen across boundaries. Values had to change throughout British Airways. People had to learn to collaborate and to develop a collective sense of responsibility for the direction and performance of the airline. Marshall identified the essential adaptive challenge: creating trust throughout the organization. He is one of the first executives we have known to make "creating trust" a priority.

To lead British Airways, Marshall had to get his executive team to understand the nature of the threat created by dissatisfied customers: Did it represent a technical challenge or an adaptive challenge? Would expert advice and technical adjustments within basic routines suffice, or would people throughout the company have to learn different ways of doing business, develop new competencies, and begin to work collectively?

Marshall and his team set out to diagnose in more detail the organization's challenges. They looked in three places. First, they listened to the ideas and concerns of people inside and outside the organization—meeting with crews on flights, showing up in the 350-person reservations center in New York, wandering around the baggage-handling area in Tokyo, or visiting the passenger lounge in whatever airport they happened to be in. Their primary questions were, Whose values, beliefs, attitudes, or behaviors would have to change in order for progress to take place? What shifts in priorities, resources, and power were necessary? What sacrifices would have to be made and by whom?

Second, Marshall and his team saw conflicts as clues—symptoms of adaptive challenges. The way conflicts across functions were being expressed were mere surface phenomena; the underlying conflicts had to be diagnosed. Disputes over seemingly technical issues such as procedures, schedules, and lines of authority were in fact proxies for underlying conflicts about values and norms.

Third, Marshall and his team held a mirror up to themselves, recognizing that they embodied the adaptive challenges facing the organization. Early in the transformation of British Airways, competing values and norms were played out on the executive team in dysfunctional ways that impaired the capacity of the rest of the company to collaborate across functions and units and make the necessary trade-offs. No executive can hide from the fact that his or her team reflects the best and the worst of the company's values and norms, and therefore provides a case in point for insight into the nature of the adaptive work ahead.

Thus, identifying its adaptive challenge was crucial in British Airways' bid to become the world's favorite airline. For the strategy to succeed, the company's leaders needed to understand themselves, their people, and the potential sources of conflict. Marshall recognized that strategy development itself requires adaptive work.

Regulate Distress

Adaptive work generates distress. Before putting people to work on challenges for which there are no ready solutions, a leader must realize that people can learn only so much so fast. At the same time, they must feel the need to change as reality brings new challenges. They cannot learn new ways when they are overwhelmed, but eliminating stress altogether removes the impetus for doing adaptive work. Because a leader must strike a delicate balance between having people feel the need to change and having them feel overwhelmed by change, leadership is a razor's edge.

A leader must attend to three fundamental tasks in order to help maintain a productive level of tension. Adhering to these tasks will allow him or her to motivate people without disabling them. First, a leader must create what can be called a *holding environment.* To use the analogy of a pressure cooker, a leader needs to regulate the pressure by turning up the heat while also allowing some steam to escape. If the pressure exceeds the cooker's capacity, the cooker can blow up. However, nothing cooks without some heat.

In the early stages of a corporate change, the holding environment can be a temporary "place" in which a leader creates the conditions for diverse groups to talk to one another about the challenges facing them, to frame and debate issues, and to clarify the assumptions behind competing perspectives and values. Over time, more issues can be phased in as they become ripe. At British Airways, for example, the shift from an internal focus to a customer focus took place over four or five years and dealt with important issues in succession: building a credible executive team, communicating with a highly fragmented organization, defining new measures of performance and compensation, and developing sophisticated information systems. During that time, employees at all levels learned to identify what and how they needed to change.

Thus, a leader must sequence and pace the work. Too often, senior managers convey that everything is important. They start new initiatives without stopping other activities, or they start too many initiatives at the same time. They overwhelm and disorient the very people who need to take responsibility for the work.

Second, a leader is responsible for direction, protection, orientation, managing conflict, and shaping norms. (See the exhibit "Adaptive work calls for leadership.") Fulfilling these responsibilities is also important for a manager in technical or routine situations. But a leader engaged in adaptive work uses his authority to fulfill them differently. A leader provides direction by identifying the organization's adaptive challenge and framing the key questions and issues. A leader protects people by managing the rate of change. A leader orients people to new roles and responsibilities by clarifying business realities and key values. A leader helps expose conflict, viewing it as the engine of creativity and learning. Finally, a leader helps the organization maintain those norms that must endure and challenge those that need to change.

Adaptive work calls for leadership

In the course of regulating people's distress, a leader faces several key responsibilities and may have to use his or her authority differently depending on the type of work situation.

Leader's responsibilities	Type of situation	
	Technical or routine	*Adaptive*
Direction	Define problems and provide solutions	Identify the adaptive challenge and frame key questions and issues
Protection	Shield the organization from external threats	Let the organization feel external pressures within a range it can stand
Orientation	Clarify roles and responsibilities	Challenge current roles and resist pressure to define new roles quickly
Managing conflict	Restore order	Expose conflict or let it emerge
Shaping norms	Maintain norms	Challenge unproductive norms

Third, a leader must have presence and poise; regulating distress is perhaps a leader's most difficult job. The pressures to restore equilibrium are enormous. Just as molecules bang hard against the walls of a pressure cooker, people bang up against leaders who are trying to sustain the pressures of tough, conflict-filled work. Although leadership demands a deep understanding of the pain of change—the fears and sacrifices associated with major readjustment—it also requires the ability to hold steady and maintain the tension. Otherwise, the pressure escapes and the stimulus for learning and change is lost.

A leader has to have the emotional capacity to tolerate uncertainty, frustration, and pain. He has to be able to raise tough questions without getting too anxious himself. Employees as well as colleagues and customers will carefully observe verbal and nonverbal cues to a leader's ability to hold steady. He needs to communicate confidence that he and they can tackle the tasks ahead.

Maintain Disciplined Attention

Different people within the same organization bring different experiences, assumptions, values, beliefs, and habits to their work. This diversity is valuable because innovation and learning are the products of differences. No one learns anything without being open to contrasting points of view. Yet managers at all levels are often unwilling—or unable—to address their competing perspectives collectively. They frequently avoid paying attention to issues that disturb them. They restore equilibrium quickly, often with work avoidance maneuvers. A leader must get employees to confront tough trade-offs in values, procedures, operating styles, and power.

That is as true at the top of the organization as it is in the middle or on the front line. Indeed, if the executive team cannot model adaptive work, the organization will languish. If senior managers can't draw out and deal with divisive issues, how will people elsewhere in the organization change their behaviors and rework their relationships? As Jan Carlzon, the legendary CEO of Scandinavian Airlines System (SAS), told us, "One of the most interesting missions of leadership is getting people on the executive team to listen to and learn from one another. Held in debate, people can learn their way to collective solutions when they understand one another's assumptions. The work of the leader is to get conflict out into the open and use it as a source of creativity."

Because work avoidance is rampant in organizations, a leader has to counteract distractions that prevent people from dealing with adaptive issues. Scapegoating, denial, focusing only on today's technical issues, or attacking individuals rather than the perspectives they represent—all forms of work avoidance—are to be expected when an organization undertakes adaptive work. Distractions have to be identified when they occur so that people will regain focus.

When sterile conflict takes the place of dialogue, a leader has to step in and put the team to work on reframing the issues. She has to deepen the debate with questions, unbundling the issues into their parts rather than letting conflict remain polarized and superficial. When people preoccupy themselves with blaming external forces, higher management, or a heavy workload, a leader has to sharpen the team's sense of responsibility for carving out the time to press forward. When the team fragments and individuals resort to protecting their own turf, leaders have to demonstrate the need for collaboration. People have to discover the value of consulting with one another and using one another as resources in the problem-solving process. For example, one CEO we know uses executive meetings, even those that focus on operational and technical issues, as opportunities to teach the team how to work collectively on adaptive problems.

Of course, only the rare manager intends to avoid adaptive work. In general, people feel ambivalent about it. Although they want to make progress on hard problems or live up to their renewed and clarified values, people also want to avoid the associated distress. Just as millions of U.S. citizens want to reduce the federal budget deficit, but not by giving up their tax dollars or benefits or jobs, so, too, managers may consider adaptive work a priority but have difficulty sacrificing their familiar ways of doing business. People need leadership to help them maintain their focus on the tough questions. Disciplined attention is the currency of leadership.

Give the Work Back to People

Everyone in the organization has special access to information that comes from his or her particular vantage point. Everyone may see different needs and opportunities. People who sense early changes in the marketplace are often at the periphery, but the organization will thrive if it can bring that information to bear on tactical and strategic decisions. When people do not act on their special knowledge, businesses fail to adapt.

All too often, people look up the chain of command, expecting senior management to meet market challenges for which they themselves are responsible. Indeed, the greater and more persistent distresses that accompany adaptive work make such dependence worse. People tend to become passive, and senior managers who pride themselves on being problem solvers take decisive action. That behavior restores equilibrium in the short term but ultimately leads to complacency and habits of work avoidance that shield people from responsibility, pain, and the need to change.

Getting people to assume greater responsibility is not easy. Not only are many lower-level employees comfortable being told what to do, but many managers are accustomed to treating subordinates like machinery that requires control. Letting people take the initiative in defining and solving problems means that management needs to learn to support rather than control. Workers, for their part, need to learn to take responsibility.

Jan Carlzon encouraged responsibility taking at SAS by trusting others and decentralizing authority. A leader has to let people bear the weight of responsibility. "The key is to let them discover the problem," he said. "You won't be successful if people aren't carrying the recognition of the problem and the solution within themselves." To that end, Carlzon sought widespread engagement.

For example, in his first two years at SAS, Carlzon spent up to 50% of his time communicating directly in large meetings and indirectly in a host of innovative ways: through workshops, brainstorming sessions, learning exercises, newsletters, brochures, and exposure in the public media. He demonstrated through a variety of symbolic acts—for example, by eliminating the pretentious executive dining room and burning thousands of pages of manuals and handbooks—the extent to which rules had come to dominate the company. He made himself a pervasive presence, meeting with and listening to people both inside and outside the organization. He even wrote a book, *Moments of Truth* (HarperCollins, 1989), to explain his values, philosophy, and strategy. As Carlzon noted, "If no one else read it, at least my people would."

A leader also must develop collective self-confidence. Again, Carlzon said it well: "People aren't born with self-confidence. Even the most self-confident people can be broken. Self-confidence comes from success, experience, and the organization's environment. The leader's most important role is to instill confidence in people. They must dare to take risks and responsibility. You must back them up if they make mistakes."

Protect Voices of Leadership from Below

Giving a voice to all people is the foundation of an organization that is willing to experiment and learn. But, in fact, whistle-blowers, creative deviants, and other such original voices routinely get smashed and silenced in organizational life. They generate disequilibrium, and the easiest way for an organization to restore equilibrium is to neutralize those voices, sometimes in the name of teamwork and "alignment."

The voices from below are usually not as articulate as one would wish. People speaking beyond their authority usually feel self-conscious and sometimes have to generate "too much" passion to get themselves geared up for speaking out. Of course, that often makes it harder for them to communicate effectively. They pick the wrong time and place, and often bypass proper channels of communication and lines of authority. But buried inside a poorly packaged interjection may lie an important intuition that needs to be teased out and considered. To toss it out for its bad timing, lack of clarity, or seeming unreasonableness is to lose potentially valuable information and discourage a potential leader in the organization.

That is what happened to David, a manager in a large manufacturing company. He had listened when his superiors encouraged people to look for problems, speak openly, and take responsibility. So he raised an issue about one of the CEO's pet projects—an issue that was deemed "too hot to handle" and had been swept under the carpet for years. Everyone understood that it was not open to discussion, but David knew that proceeding with the project could damage or derail key elements of the company's overall strategy. He raised the issue directly in a meeting with his boss and the CEO. He provided a clear description of the problem, a rundown of competing perspectives, and a summary of the consequences of continuing to pursue the project.

The CEO angrily squelched the discussion and reinforced the positive aspects of his pet project. When David and his boss left the room, his boss exploded: "Who do you think you are, with your holier-than-thou attitude?" He insinuated that David had never liked the CEO's pet project because David hadn't come up with the idea himself. The subject was closed.

David had greater expertise in the area of the project than either his boss or the CEO. But his two superiors demonstrated no curiosity, no effort to investigate David's reasoning, no awareness that he was behaving responsibly with the interests of the company at heart. It rapidly became clear to David that it was more important to understand what mattered to the boss than to focus on real issues. The CEO and David's boss together squashed the viewpoint of a leader from below and thereby killed his potential for leadership in the organization. He would either leave the company or never go against the grain again.

Leaders must rely on others within the business to raise questions that may indicate an impending adaptive challenge. They have to provide cover to people who point to the internal contradictions of the enterprise. Those individuals often have the perspective to provoke rethinking that people in authority do not. Thus, as a rule of thumb, when authority figures feel the reflexive urge to glare at or otherwise silence someone, they should resist. The urge to restore social equilibrium is quite powerful, and it comes on fast. One has to get accustomed to getting on the balcony, delaying the impulse, and asking, What is this guy really talking about? Is there something we're missing?

Doing Adaptive Work at KPMG Netherlands

The highly successful KPMG Netherlands provides a good example of how a company can engage in adaptive work. In 1994, Ruud Koedijk, the firm's chairman, recognized a strategic challenge. Although the auditing, consulting, and tax-preparation partnership was the industry leader in the Netherlands and was highly profitable, growth opportunities in the segments it served were limited. Margins in the auditing business were being squeezed as the market became more saturated, and competition in the consulting business was increasing as well. Koedijk knew that the firm needed to move into more profitable growth areas, but he didn't know what they were or how KPMG might identify them.

Koedijk and his board were confident that they had the tools to do the analytical strategy work: analyze trends and discontinuities, understand core competencies, assess their competitive position, and map potential opportunities. They were considerably less certain that they could commit to implementing the strategy that would emerge from their work. Historically, the partnership had resisted attempts to change, basically because the partners were content with the way things were. They had been successful for a long time, so they saw no reason to learn new ways of doing business, either from their fellow partners or from anyone lower down in the organization. Overturning the partners' attitude and its deep impact on the organization's culture posed an enormous adaptive challenge for KPMG.

Koedijk could see from the balcony that the very structure of KPMG inhibited change. In truth, KPMG was less a partnership than a collection of small fiefdoms in which each partner was a lord. The firm's success was the cumulative accomplishment of each of the individual partners, not the unified result of 300 colleagues pulling together toward a shared ambition. Success was measured solely in terms of the profitability of individual units. As one partner described it, "If the bottom line was correct, you were a 'good fellow.'" As a result, one partner would not trespass on another's turf, and learning from others was a rare event. Because independence was so highly valued, confrontations were rare and conflict was camouflaged. If partners wanted to resist firmwide change, they did not kill the issue directly. "Say yes, do no" was the operative phrase.

Koedijk also knew that this sense of autonomy got in the way of developing new talent at KPMG. Directors rewarded their subordinates for two things: not making mistakes and delivering a high number of billable hours per week. The emphasis was not on creativity or innovation. Partners were looking for errors when they reviewed their subordinates' work, not for new understanding or fresh insight. Although Koedijk could see the broad outlines of the adaptive challenges facing his organization, he knew that he could not mandate behavioral change. What he could do was create the conditions for people to discover for themselves how they needed to change. He set a process in motion to make that happen.

To start, Koedijk held a meeting of all 300 partners and focused their attention on the history of KPMG, the current business reality, and the business issues they could expect to face. He then raised the question of how they would go about changing as a firm and asked for their perspectives on the issues. By launching the strategic initiative through dialogue rather than edict, he built trust within the partner ranks. Based on this emerging trust and his own credibility, Koedijk persuaded the partners to release 100 partners and nonpartners from their day-to-day responsibilities to work on the strategic challenges. They would devote 60% of their time for nearly four months to that work.

Koedijk and his colleagues established a strategic integration team of 12 senior partners to work with the 100 professionals (called "the 100") from different levels and disciplines. Engaging people below the rank of partner in a major strategic initiative was unheard of and signaled a new approach from the start: Many of these people's opinions had never before been valued or sought by authority figures in the firm. Divided into 14 task forces, the 100 were to work in three areas: gauging future trends and discontinuities, defining core competencies, and grappling with the adaptive challenges facing the organization. They were housed on a separate floor with their own support staff, and they were unfettered by traditional rules and regulations. Hennie Both, KPMG's director of marketing and communications, signed on as project manager.

As the strategy work got under way, the task forces had to confront the existing KPMG culture. Why? Because they literally could not do their new work within the old rules. They could not work when strong respect for the individual came at the expense of effective teamwork, when deeply held individual beliefs got in the way of genuine discussion, and when unit loyalties formed a barrier to cross-functional problem solving. Worst of all, task force members found themselves avoiding conflict and unable to discuss those problems. A number of the task forces became dysfunctional and unable to do their strategy work.

To focus their attention on what needed to change, Both helped the task forces map the culture they desired against the current culture. They discovered very little overlap. The top descriptors of the current culture were: develop opposing views, demand perfection, and avoid conflict. The top characteristics of the desired culture were: create the opportunity for self-fulfillment, develop a caring environment, and maintain trusting relations with colleagues. Articulating this gap made tangible for the group the adaptive challenge that Koedijk saw facing KPMG. In other words, the people who needed to do the changing had finally framed the adaptive challenge for themselves: How could KPMG succeed at a competence-based strategy that depended on cooperation across multiple units and layers if its people couldn't succeed in these task forces? Armed with that understanding, the task force members could become emissaries to the rest of the firm.

On a more personal level, each member was asked to identify his or her individual adaptive challenge. What attitudes, behaviors, or habits did each one need to change, and what specific actions would he or she take? Who else needed to be involved for individual change to take root? Acting as coaches and consultants, the task force members gave one another supportive feedback and suggestions. They had learned to confide, to listen, and to advise with genuine care.

Progress on these issues raised the level of trust dramatically, and task force members began to understand what adapting their behavior meant in everyday terms. They understood how to identify an adaptive issue and developed a language with which to discuss what they needed to do to improve their collective ability to solve problems. They talked about dialogue, work avoidance, and using the collective intelligence of the group. They knew how to call one another on dysfunctional behavior. They had begun to develop the culture required to implement the new business strategy.

Despite the critical breakthroughs toward developing a collective understanding of the adaptive challenge, regulating the level of distress was a constant preoccupation for Koedijk, the board, and Both. The nature of the work was distressing. Strategy work means broad assignments with limited instructions; at KPMG, people were accustomed to highly structured assignments. Strategy work also means being creative. At one breakfast meeting, a board member stood on a table to challenge the group to be more creative and toss aside old rules. This radical and unexpected behavior further raised the distress level: No one had ever seen a partner behave this way before. People realized that their work experience had prepared them only for performing routine tasks with people "like them" from their own units.

The process allowed for conflict and focused people's attention on the hot issues in order to help them learn how to work with conflict in a constructive manner. But the heat was kept within a tolerable range in some of the following ways:

- On one occasion when tensions were unusually high, the 100 were brought together to voice their concerns to the board in an Oprah Winfrey–style meeting. The board sat in the center of an auditorium and took pointed questions from the surrounding group.

- The group devised sanctions to discourage unwanted behavior. In the soccer-crazy Netherlands, all participants in the process were issued the yellow cards that soccer referees use to indicate "foul" to offending players. They used the cards to stop the action when someone started arguing his or her point without listening to or understanding the assumptions and competing perspectives of other participants.

- The group created symbols. They compared the old KPMG to a hippopotamus that was large and cumbersome, liked to sleep a lot, and became aggressive when its normal habits were disturbed. They aspired to be dolphins, which they characterized as playful, eager to learn, and happily willing to go the extra mile for the team. They even paid attention to the statement that clothes make: It surprised some clients to see managers wandering through the KPMG offices that summer in Bermuda shorts and T-shirts.

- The group made a deliberate point of having fun. "Playtime" could mean long bicycle rides or laser-gun games at a local amusement center. In one spontaneous moment at the KPMG offices, a discussion of the power of people mobilized toward a common goal led the group to go outside and use their collective leverage to move a seemingly immovable concrete block.

- The group attended frequent two- and three-day off-site meetings to help bring closure to parts of the work.

These actions, taken as a whole, altered attitudes and behaviors. Curiosity became more valued than obedience to rules. People no longer deferred to the senior authority figure in the room; genuine dialogue neutralized hierarchical power in the battle over ideas. The tendency for each individual to promote his or her pet solution gave way to understanding other perspectives. A confidence in the ability of people in different units to work together and work things out emerged. The people with the most curious minds and interesting questions soon became the most respected.

As a result of confronting strategic and adaptive challenges, KPMG as a whole will move from auditing to assurance, from operations consulting to shaping corporate vision, from business-process reengineering to developing organizational capabilities, and from teaching traditional skills to its own clients to creating learning organizations. The task forces identified $50 million to $60 million worth of new business opportunities.

Many senior partners who had believed that a firm dominated by the auditing mentality could not contain creative people were surprised when the process unlocked creativity, passion, imagination, and a willingness to take risks. Two stories illustrate the fundamental changes that took place in the firm's mind-set.

We saw one middle manager develop the confidence to create a new business. He spotted the opportunity to provide KPMG services to virtual organizations and strategic alliances. He traveled the world, visiting the leaders of 65 virtual organizations. The results of his innovative research served as a resource to KPMG in entering this growing market. Moreover, he represented the new KPMG by giving a keynote address discussing his findings at a world forum. We also saw a 28-year-old female auditor skillfully guide a group of older, male senior partners through a complex day of looking at opportunities associated with implementing the firm's new strategies. That could not have occurred the year before. The senior partners never would have listened to such a voice from below.

Leadership as Learning

Many efforts to transform organizations through mergers and acquisitions, restructuring, reengineering, and strategy work falter because managers fail to grasp the requirements of adaptive work. They make the classic error of treating adaptive challenges like technical problems that can be solved by tough-minded senior executives.

The implications of that error go to the heart of the work of leaders in organizations today. Leaders crafting strategy have access to the technical expertise and the tools they need to calculate the benefits of a merger or restructuring, understand future trends and discontinuities, identify opportunities, map existing competencies, and identify the steering mechanisms to support their strategic direction. These tools and techniques are readily available both within organizations and from a variety of consulting firms, and they are very useful. In many cases, however, seemingly good strategies fail to be implemented. And often the failure is misdiagnosed: "We had a good strategy, but we couldn't execute it effectively."

In fact, the strategy itself is often deficient because too many perspectives were ignored during its formulation. The failure to do the necessary adaptive work during the strategy development process is a symptom of senior managers' technical orientation. Managers frequently derive their solution to a problem and then try to sell it to some colleagues and bypass or sandbag others in the commitment-building process. Too often, leaders, their team, and consultants fail to identify and tackle the adaptive dimensions of the challenge and to ask themselves, Who needs to learn what in order to develop, understand, commit to, and implement the strategy?

The same technical orientation entraps business-process-reengineering and restructuring initiatives, in which consultants and managers have the know-how to do the technical work of framing the objectives, designing a new work flow, documenting and communicating results, and identifying the activities to be performed by people in the organization. In many instances, reengineering falls short of the mark because it treats process redesign as a technical problem: Managers neglect to identify the adaptive work and involve the people who have to do the changing. Senior executives fail to invest their time and their souls in understanding these issues and guiding people through the transition. Indeed, engineering is itself the wrong metaphor.

In short, the prevailing notion that leadership consists of having a vision and aligning people with that vision is bankrupt because it continues to treat adaptive situations as if they were technical: The authority figure is supposed to divine where the company is going, and people are supposed to follow. Leadership is reduced to a combination of grand knowing and salesmanship. Such a perspective reveals a basic misconception about the way businesses succeed in addressing adaptive challenges. Adaptive situations are hard to define and resolve precisely because they demand the work and responsibility of managers and people throughout the organization. They are not amenable to solutions provided by leaders; adaptive solutions require members of the organization to take responsibility for the problematic situations that face them.

Leadership has to take place every day. It cannot be the responsibility of the few, a rare event, or a once-in-a-lifetime opportunity. In our world, in our businesses, we face adaptive challenges all the time. When an executive is asked to square conflicting aspirations, he and his people face an adaptive challenge. When a manager sees a solution to a problem—technical in many respects except that it requires a change in the attitudes and habits of subordinates—he faces an adaptive challenge. When an employee close to the front line sees a gap between the organization's purpose and the objectives he is asked to achieve, he faces both an adaptive challenge and the risks and opportunity of leading from below.

Leadership, as seen in this light, requires a learning strategy. A leader, from above or below, with or without authority, has to engage people in confronting the challenge, adjusting their values, changing perspectives, and learning new habits. To an authoritative person who prides himself on his ability to tackle hard problems, this shift may come as a rude awakening. But it also should ease the burden of having to know all the answers and bear all the load. To the person who waits to receive either the coach's call or "the vision" to lead, this change may also seem a mixture of good news and bad news. The adaptive demands of our time require leaders who take responsibility without waiting for revelation or request. One can lead with no more than a question in hand.

Originally published in January 1997. Reprint R0111K

Teamwork on the Fly

How to Master the New Art
of Teaming. *by Amy C. Edmondson*

IF YOU WATCHED the Beijing 2008 Olympic Games, you probably marveled at the Water Cube: that magnificent 340,000-square-foot box framed in steel and covered with semitransparent, ecoefficient blue bubbles. Formally named the Beijing National Aquatics Center, the Water Cube hosted swimming and diving events, could hold 17,000 spectators, won prestigious engineering and design awards, and cost an estimated 10.2 billion yuan. The structure was the joint effort of global design and engineering company Arup, PTW Architects, the China State Construction Engineering Corporation (CSCEC), China Construction Design International, and dozens of contractors and consultants. The goal was clear: Build an iconic structure to reflect Chinese culture, integrate with the site, and minimize energy consumption—on time and within budget. But how to do all that was less clear.

Ultimately, Tristram Carfrae, an Arup structural engineer based in Sydney, corralled dozens of people from 20 disciplines and four countries to win the competition and deliver the building. This required more than traditional project management. Success depended on bridging dramatically different national, organizational, and occupational cultures to collaborate in fluid groupings that emerged and dissolved in response to needs that were identified as the work progressed.

The Water Cube was an unusual endeavor, but the strategy employed to complete it—a strategy I call *teaming*—epitomizes the new era of business. Teaming is teamwork on the fly: a pickup basketball game rather than plays run by a team that has trained as a unit for years. It's a way to gather experts in temporary groups to solve problems they're encountering for the first and perhaps only time. Think of clinicians in an emergency room, who convene quickly to solve a specific patient problem and then move on to address other cases with different colleagues, compared with a surgical team that performs the same procedure under highly controlled conditions day after day. When companies need to accomplish something that hasn't been done before, and might not be done again, traditional team structures aren't practical. It's just not possible to identify the right skills and knowledge in advance and to trust that circumstances will not change. Under those conditions, a leader's emphasis has to shift from composing and managing teams to inspiring and enabling teaming.

Stable teams of people who have learned over time to work well together can be powerful tools. But given the speed of change, the intensity of market competition, and the unpredictability of customers' needs today, there often isn't enough time to build that kind of team. Instead, organizations increasingly must bring together not only their own far-flung employees from various disciplines and divisions but also external specialists and stakeholders, only to disband them when they've achieved their goal or when a new opportunity arises. More and more people in nearly every industry and type of company are now working on multiple teams that vary in duration, have a constantly shifting membership, and pursue moving targets. Product design, patient care, strategy development, pharmaceutical research, and rescue operations are just a few of the domains in which teaming is essential.

This evolution of teamwork presents serious challenges. In fact, it can lead to chaos. But employees and organizations that learn how to team well—by embracing several project management and team leadership principles—can reap important benefits. Teaming helps individuals acquire knowledge, skills, and networks. And it lets

Idea in Brief

In today's fast-moving, ultracompetitive global business environment, you can't rely on stable teams to get the work done. Instead, you need "teaming."

Teaming is flexible teamwork. It's a way to gather experts from far-flung divisions and disciplines into temporary groups to tackle unexpected problems and identify emerging opportunities. It's happening now in nearly every industry and type of company.

To "team" well, employees and organizations must embrace principles of **project management**—such as scoping out the project, structuring the group, and sorting tasks by level of interdependence—and of **team leadership,** such as emphasizing purpose, building psychological safety, and embracing failure and conflict.

Those who master teaming will reap benefits. Teaming allows individuals to acquire knowledge, skills, and networks, and it lets companies accelerate the delivery of current offerings while responding quickly to new challenges. Teaming is a way to get work done while figuring out how to do it better.

companies accelerate the delivery of current products and services while responding quickly to new opportunities. Teaming is a way to get work done while figuring out how to do it better; it's executing and learning at the same time.

From Teams to Teaming

The stable project teams we grew up with still work beautifully in many contexts. By pulling together the right people with the right combination of skills and training and giving them time to build trust, companies can accomplish big things. For instance, traditional teams at Simmons Bedding Company in the early 2000s achieved a major turnaround by driving waste out of operations, energizing sales, and building better relationships with dealers. In those teams, membership was clearly defined, each group knew which part of the operation it was responsible for, and no one had to do fundamentally new types of work. These stable teams left a trail of positive indicators, including savings of $21 million in operational costs without layoffs in the first year alone; increased sales and customer satisfaction; and dramatically improved employee morale. But Simmons had what many companies today lack: reasonably stable customer preferences, purely domestic operations, and no significant boundaries that had to be crossed to get the job done.

Situations that call for teaming are, by contrast, complex and uncertain, full of unexpected events that require rapid changes in course. No two projects are alike, so people must get up to speed quickly on brand-new topics, again and again. Because solutions can come from anywhere, team members do, too. As a result, teaming requires people to cross boundaries, which can be risky. Experts from different functions—operating with their own jargon, norms, and knowledge—often clash. People who aren't from the same division or organization can have competing values and priorities. When junior and senior staff members from different divisions are paired, reporting structures and hierarchies often silence dissent. On global teams, time zone differences and electronic correspondence can give rise to miscommunication and logistical snafus. And because the work relationships are temporary, investing the time to grow accustomed to new colleagues' work styles, strengths, and weaknesses isn't possible.

Disagreements were plentiful in designing the Water Cube, given the need for intense collaboration across boundaries. Early on, two architecture firms—one Chinese and one Australian—each developed a design concept. One was a wave-shaped structure, and the other was an eroded rectangular form. A participant recalled tension between what felt like two camps. Another added, "It was like two design processes were going on at the same time. One team was working secretly on its idea, and the other architects were doing their own thing."

Consider also a geographically distributed product development team I studied in a high-tech materials company. Working to develop a custom polymer for a Japanese manufacturer's new-product launch, the group nearly broke down over conflicting cultural norms about customer relationships. One team member, a U.S.-based marketing expert, wanted data on the manufacturer's market strategy to assess the longer-term opportunity for the polymer; she was deeply frustrated by a Japanese team member's failure to fulfill her request. In turn, the Japanese team member, an engineer, thought the U.S. marketer was pushy and unsupportive. She knew that the customer had not yet established a strategy for the product and that demanding more information at this stage in the nascent relationship would cause the customer to "lose face."

At the same company, another team of seven experts spread across five facilities on three continents was trying to develop a different polymer on an aggressive timetable. In spite of its combined knowledge, the group reached a dead end in an effort to source a specialized compound. One member eventually found a colleague from outside the formal team who could produce it. In technologically and scientifically complex projects like this one, teaming occurs not just across the boundaries it was designed to span but also across boundaries between projects, when colleagues with expertise and goodwill help out.

As these brief examples illustrate, teaming involves both technical and interpersonal challenges. It therefore falls to leaders to draw on best practices of project management (to plan and execute in a complex and changing environment) and team leadership (to foster collaboration in shifting groups that will be inherently prone to conflict). This is the hardware and the software of teaming. Let's tackle the hardware first.

The Hardware

To facilitate effective teaming, leaders need to manage the technical issues of *scoping* out the challenge, lightly *structuring* the boundaries, and *sorting* tasks for execution. A classic error is assuming that everything a team does has to be collaborative. Instead, input and interaction should be used as needed so that not all tasks become team encounters, which are time-consuming. Another error is subjecting highly uncertain initiatives to traditional project management tools that cope with complexity by dividing work into predictable phases such as initiation, planning, execution, completion, and monitoring. The hardware of teaming modifies those tools to enable execution during, rather than after, learning and planning.

Scoping

The first step in any teaming scenario is to draw a line in the (shifting) sand by scoping out the challenge, determining what expertise is needed, tapping collaborators, and outlining roles and responsibilities. Leaders of the Water Cube project, for example, started by identifying a handful of Pacific Rim firms that were capable of state-of-the-art engineering and design and willing to work together. In other organizations, this scouting activity might involve lateral and vertical searches through the hierarchy to identify people with relevant expertise. When a team is already assembled, scoping includes figuring out what additional resources are needed, as occurred in the second polymer team, or which team members can be freed up over time to join other groups. Successful scoping articulates the best possible current definition of the work and acknowledges that the definition will evolve along with the project.

Structuring

The second step is to offer some structure—figurative scaffolding—to help the team function effectively. In building, a scaffold is a light, temporary structure that supports the process of construction. For improvisational, interdependent work carried out by a shifting mix of participants, some structuring can help the group by establishing boundaries and targets. Scaffolding in a teaming situation could include a list of team members that contains pertinent biographical and professional information; a shared radio frequency, chat room, or intranet; visits to teammates' facilities; or temporary shared office space. The use of "shirts" and "skins" to designate sides in a pickup basketball game is a kind of scaffold, as is a quick briefing at the launch of a rescue mission that assigns, say, groups of four people, each with a different role, to head in three different directions. The objective of structuring is to make it easier for teaming partners to coordinate and communicate—face-to-face or virtually.

Melissa Valentine, a doctoral candidate at Harvard University, and I recently looked at the use of figurative scaffolds in emergency rooms, where fast-paced teaming has life-or-death consequences. In this setting, physicians, nurses, and technicians with constantly varying schedules depend on one another to make good patient care decisions and execute them flawlessly in real time. More often than not, people scheduled on the same shift do not have long-standing work relationships and may not even know one another's names. Valentine and I found several hospitals that were experimenting with a system to make ad hoc collaboration easier by dividing ERs into subsections ("pods") incorporating a preset mix of roles (such as an attending physician, three nurses, a resident, and an intern) into which clinicians slide when they come to work. As a result, the teaming arrangement for each shift is established early on, which reduces coordination time, boosts accountability, improves operational efficiency, and shortens patient waits.

Temporary colocation is a common type of scaffold for high-priority, short-term projects in corporate settings. Motorola used this for one of the most successful product launches in history: the RAZR mobile phone. Battling fierce global competition in 2003, the company set out to create the thinnest phone ever in record time. Roger Jellicoe, an electrical engineer, led the project, in which 20 engineers and other experts from various groups and locations temporarily worked side by side in an otherwise unremarkable facility an hour from Chicago. The resulting product, introduced in 2004, was a stunning market success: More than 110 million RAZRs were sold in the first four years.

Sorting
The third step is the conscious prioritizing of tasks according to the degree of interdependence among individuals. As the organizational theorist James Thompson noted a half century ago, organizations exist to combine people's efforts. Combining, or interdependence, can take three forms: pooled, sequential, or reciprocal. *Pooled* interdependence was the very essence of the industrial era—breaking work down into small tasks that could be done and monitored individually, without input from others. To the extent that such work exists in current projects, there's flexibility in when and where it gets done. But most tasks now require some degree of interaction among individuals or subgroups.

Sequential interdependence characterizes tasks that need input (information, material, or both) from someone else. The assembly line is the classic example: Unless the guy upstream does his part, I cannot do mine. Teaming situations are full of these tasks; they must be scheduled carefully to avoid delays. Effective teaming streamlines handoffs between sequential tasks to avoid wasted time and miscommunication. Too often, people focus on their own part of the work and assume that if others do likewise, that will be sufficient for good performance.

The management of tasks involving *reciprocal* interdependence—work that calls for back-and-forth communication and mutual adjustment—is most critical to successful teaming. Because it's often difficult for people in cross-functional, fluid groups to reach consensus, these tasks tend to become bottlenecks. They should therefore be prioritized. It's crucial that leaders specify points when individuals or subgroups must gather—literally or virtually—to coordinate upcoming decisions and resources or to analyze and solve problems.

One factor that distinguished the design and construction of the Water Cube from most large-scale building projects—in which different tasks are performed sequentially by different disciplines—was that all the experts came together at the beginning to brainstorm and consider the implications of various design ideas. This decision about process deliberately converted traditionally sequential activities into reciprocal ones. The result was greater complexity and more need for coordination but also better design, less waste, quicker completion, and lower cost. One outcome was the radical decision to use ethylene tetrafluoroethylene (ETFE), a material that had been developed for space exploration but never used in a major building. Its unique properties solved several acoustic, structural, and lighting problems, and although the choice initially appeared risky, Arup engineers used the latest computer modeling software to confirm the safety of ETFE for their purposes and to communicate their thinking to the Chinese authorities.

Of course not all tasks in the Water Cube project required reciprocal interdependence. Expert subgroups had many independent

The Behaviors of Successful Teaming

- Speaking up: Communicating honestly and directly with others by asking questions, acknowledging errors, raising issues, and explaining ideas

- Experimenting: Taking an iterative approach to action that recognizes the novelty and uncertainty inherent in interactions between individuals and in the possibilities and plans they develop

- Reflecting: Observing, questioning, and discussing processes and outcomes on a consistent basis—daily, weekly, monthly—that reflects the rhythm of the work

- Listening intently: Working hard to understand the knowledge, expertise, ideas, and opinions of others

- Integrating: Synthesizing different facts and points of view to create new possibilities

tasks, such as fire safety analyses and certain technical drawings. But for interdependent work, groups had to coordinate across what the company called "interfaces." Carfrae and his colleagues divided the entire project into "volumes" (separable parts) on the basis of areas of interdependence and assigned subteams to carry them out. When issues required coordination across volumes, interface coordination meetings were held—for just the relevant parties—to manage the structural, organizational, or procedural boundaries. In this way, the project eliminated mistakes that might otherwise occur at such boundaries—saving materials, costs, and headaches.

The Software

The hardware of teaming rarely works smoothly unless the software is thoughtfully managed as well. (See "The Behaviors of Successful Teaming.") One challenge of any kind of teamwork is that people working together are more vulnerable to the effects of others' decisions and actions than people working independently. Stable teams overcome this by giving members time to get to know and trust one another, which makes it easier to speak up, listen closely, and interact fluidly. But constantly shifting relationships heighten the challenge. The software of teaming asks people to get comfortable with a new way of working rather than with a new set of colleagues. This new way of working requires them to act as if they trust one another—even though they don't. Of course they don't; they don't yet know one another. Leaders have at their disposal four software tools: emphasizing purpose, building psychological safety, embracing failure, and putting conflict to work.

Emphasizing purpose

Articulating what's at stake is a basic leadership tool for motivation in almost any setting, but it's particularly important in contexts that require teaming. Purpose is fundamentally about shared values; it answers the question why we (this company, this project) exist, which can galvanize even the most diverse, amorphous team. Emphasizing purpose is necessary even when the purpose is obvious, such as in the historic 70-day rescue operation of 33 Chilean miners in 2010. Andre Sougarret, the senior engineer at the Codelco mining company who led the complex rescue, constantly reminded the dozens of engineers and geologists teaming with him about the human lives they were trying to save. This helped experts from disparate disciplines, companies, and countries quickly resolve disagreements and support one another instead of competing to come up with the idea that would save the day. Jellicoe and the Motorola RAZR team emphasized producing a groundbreaking product that would be beautiful as well as practical, while the polymer developers had a mandate to satisfy their customers' needs as quickly and effectively as they could.

Building psychological safety

In fast-paced, cross-disciplinary, cross-border teaming situations, it's not necessarily easy for people to rapidly share relevant information about their ideas and expertise. Some people worry about what others will think of them. Some fear that they will be less valuable if they give away what they know. Others are reluctant to show off. Even receiving knowledge can be difficult if it feels like an admission of weakness.

Because these vital interpersonal exchanges don't always happen spontaneously, leaders must facilitate them by creating a climate of psychological safety in which it's expected that people will speak up and disagree. A basic way to create such a climate is to model the behaviors on which teaming depends: asking thoughtful questions, acknowledging ignorance about a topic or area of expertise, and conveying awareness of one's own fallibility. Leaders who act this way make it safer for everyone else to do so. To establish a psychologically safe environment for the rescue operation in Chile, Sougarret shielded everyone involved from the media, asked questions and listened carefully to people regardless of rank, and demonstrated deep interest in new ideas about how to save the miners. In the Water Cube project, Carfrae created what team members referred to as a "safe design environment" by reinforcing the need to experiment with wild ideas.

Embracing failure

Teaming necessarily leads to failures, even on the way to extraordinary successes. These failures provide essential information that guides the next steps, creating an imperative to learn from them.

In teaming situations, leaders must ensure that all participants get over their natural desire to avoid the embarrassment and loss of confidence associated with making mistakes. The RAZR team confronted failure when, despite long working hours, it missed its ambitious deadline and the associated holiday sales. Fully supported by senior management, the team launched a few months later, and the phone's sales still surpassed expectations. The first polymer team described above undertook a series of experiments that went nowhere and ultimately brought in some specialists, confident that those colleagues would not think less of them. Teaming is needed for just those kinds of situations—when the people responsible for implementing solutions are not necessarily the ones who can come up with them.

Putting conflict to work

When teaming occurs across diverse cultures, priorities, or values, progress-thwarting conflicts are common—even when leaders have done all the right things. To move forward, all parties must be pushed to consider the degree to which their positions reflect not just facts but also personal values and biases, to explain how they have arrived at their views, and to express interest in one another's analytic journeys. In this way, people can put conflict to good use.

As Chris Argyris wrote in the HBR article "Teaching Smart People How to Learn" (May 1991), learning from conflict requires us to balance our natural tendency toward advocacy (explaining, communicating, teaching) with a less spontaneous behavior: inquiry (expressions of curiosity followed by genuine listening). A useful discipline for leaders is to force moments of reflection, asking themselves and then others, "Is this the only way to see the situation? What might I be missing?" Such exploration—even in the face of deadlines—is critical to successful teaming. In fact, in my research and consulting I've found that "taking the time" to do this actually takes less time than allowing conflicts to follow their natural course.

Conflict can feel like a failure. It can be frustrating not to see eye-to-eye with collaborators, but differences of perspective are a core reason for teamwork in the first place, and resolving them effectively gives rise to new opportunities. Instead of parting ways when they disagreed about the design for the Olympic aquatics center, the Chinese and Australian designers came up with a brand-new concept that excited both sides. Would either of their original design concepts have won the competition? We can't answer that, but the new, shared solution—the Water Cube—was spectacular. Project leaders facilitated this successful outcome by assigning those rare specialists who had deep familiarity with both Chinese and Western culture to spend time in each other's firms helping to bridge differences in language, norms, practices, and expectations.

Challenges Bring Benefits

Having studied the evolution of teamwork for 20 years, I believe that teaming is not just something individuals and companies have to do now but something they should want to do now, because it's an important driver of personal and organizational development.

When managed effectively, teaming can generate not only amazing short-term results, as illustrated by the RAZR and the Water Cube, but also long-term dividends (see Table 6-1). Organizations that learn to team well become nimbler and more innovative. They are able to solve complex, cross-disciplinary problems, align divisions and employees by developing stronger and more-unified corporate cultures, deliver a wide variety of products and services, and manage unexpected events. Teaming helps companies execute even as they learn on multiple fronts, which in turn leads to improved execution.

Individuals also benefit from serial teaming, developing broader knowledge, better interpersonal skills, a bigger network of potential collaborators, and a better understanding of their company and the different cultures at work in it. In a study of product development teams, my colleagues and I found that people who had worked on teams with greater task novelty and product complexity, more-diverse colleagues, and more boundary spanning learned more than people on teams that faced fewer of those challenges.

The multinational food company Group Danone believes so strongly in the power of teaming that the company has institutionalized it in the form of Networking Attitude, a program initiated by the executives Franck Mougin and Benedikt Benenati. It encourages ad hoc projects involving employees spread across hundreds of business units that previously operated independently, with little or no cross-pollination. Using a mix of face-to-face "knowledge marketplaces" and electronically mediated discussions, managers with an interest in a particular issue, brand, or problem can find partners with whom to share practices and launch new initiatives. An internal report featured stories of 33 practices transferred across sites, from which the company expects new teams and projects to bubble up. One initiative involved a dessert Danone Brazil helped Danone France launch in under three months in response to a competitor's move; it became a €20 million business. The company now has more than 60 new "networks"—porous communities of teaming colleagues—around the globe. Networking Attitude was designed to produce business successes, and it did. But, just as important, it

TABLE 6-1

The Rewards of Teaming

The most challenging attributes of teaming can also yield big organizational and individual benefits.

Multiple functions must work together	People are geographically dispersed	Relationships are temporary	No two projects are alike	The work can be uncertain and chaotic
CHALLENGES				
Conflict can arise among people with differing values, norms, jargon, and expertise.	Time zone differences and electronic communication present logistical hurdles.	People may not have time to build trust and mutual understanding.	Individuals must get up to speed on brand-new topics quickly, again and again.	Fluid situations require constant communication and coordination.
BENEFITS				
Organizational • Innovation from combining skills and perspectives • Ability to solve cross-disciplinary problems	**Organizational** • Greater alignment across divisions • Better diffusion of the company's culture	**Organizational** • More shared experience among colleagues • Greater camaraderie across the company	**Organizational** • Ability to meet changing customer needs	**Organizational** • Ability to manage unexpected events
Individual • Boundary-spanning skills • Understanding of other disciplines • Broader perspective on the business	**Individual** • Familiarity with people in different locations • Deeper understanding of different cultures and of the organization's operations	**Individual** • Interpersonal skills • Extensive network of collaborators	**Individual** • Flexibility and agility • Ability to import ideas from one context to another	**Individual** • Project management skills • Experimentation skills

shifted a culture of localized, hierarchical decision making to one of horizontal collaboration.

_____

Teaming is more chaotic than traditional teamwork, but it is here to stay. Projects increasingly require information and process sophistication from many fields. And managers are dependent on all kinds of specialists to make decisions and get work done. To excel in a complex and uncertain business environment, people need to work together in new and unpredictable ways. That's why successful teaming starts with an embrace of the unknown and a commitment to learning that drives employees to absorb, and sometimes create, new knowledge while executing.

Originally published in April 2012. Reprint R1204D

Who Has the D?

How Clear Decision Roles Enhance Organizational
Performance. *by Paul Rogers and Marcia Blenko*

DECISIONS ARE THE COIN of the realm in business. Every success, every mishap, every opportunity seized or missed is the result of a decision that someone made or failed to make. At many companies, decisions routinely get stuck inside the organization like loose change. But it's more than loose change that's at stake, of course; it's the performance of the entire organization. Never mind what industry you're in, how big and well known your company may be, or how clever your strategy is. If you can't make the right decisions quickly and effectively, and execute those decisions consistently, your business will lose ground.

Indeed, making good decisions and making them happen quickly are the hallmarks of high-performing organizations. When we surveyed executives at 350 global companies about their organizational effectiveness, only 15% said that they have an organization that helps the business outperform competitors. What sets those top performers apart is the quality, speed, and execution of their decision making. The most effective organizations score well on the major strategic decisions—which markets to enter or exit, which businesses to buy or sell, where to allocate capital and talent. But they truly shine when it comes to the critical operating decisions requiring consistency and speed—how to drive product innovation, the best way to position brands, how to manage channel partners.

A Bit of Context

As integrated delivery systems became more common during the 1990s, a few jokes reliably got laughs among people in health care. One was: "A vote of 1,500 physicians to 1 is a tie." Another was: "For any issue, we have six committees that can say no and no committee that can say yes." Indeed, when health care provider organizations were starting to bring together physicians and hospitals, leaders needed to concern themselves primarily with getting many stakeholders on board and keeping them all happy enough to stay on board.

Those jokes don't seem so funny anymore. The pressures to perform—and to outperform competitors—now are more pressing than the pressures to keep the peace, and instead of diffusing or dodging difficult decisions, health care leaders must make and execute them. The result is that health care leaders have gone from reading this article and passing it around to actually implementing its recommendations.

For evidence that change is really afoot, look at the evolution of governance structures of larger systems, such as Providence St. Joseph Health, which has more than 50 hospitals and 800 clinics in the western United States. Increasingly, boards at systems like this are the true decision-making structures, and boards at an entity level (for example, hospital) are advisory only. Twenty years ago, provider consolidation was associated with governance ambiguity, but now consolidation is accelerating governance clarity, since the larger and more complex the organization, the greater the need for a clear strategy to make the whole greater than the sum of its parts.

The RAPID decision model described in this article may be difficult to implement in complex, still-evolving health care organizations, but worth considering as a direction for that evolution. Health care organizations that can move toward it will make strategic decisions more quickly—and make fewer wry jokes about their inability to do so.

—Thomas H. Lee

Even in companies respected for their decisiveness, however, there can be ambiguity over who is accountable for which decisions. As a result, the entire decision-making process can stall, usually at one of four bottlenecks: global versus local, center versus business unit, function versus function, and inside versus outside partners.

Idea in Brief

Decisions are the coin of the realm in business. Every success, every mishap, every opportunity seized or missed stems from a decision someone made—or failed to make. Yet in many firms, decisions routinely stall inside the organization—hurting the entire company's performance.

The culprit? Ambiguity over who's accountable for which decisions. In one auto manufacturer that was missing milestones for rolling out new models, marketers *and* product developers each thought they were responsible for deciding new models' standard features and colors. Result? Conflict over who had final say, endless revisiting of decisions—and missed deadlines that led to lost sales.

How to clarify decision accountability? Assign clear roles for the decisions that most affect your firm's performance—such as which markets to enter, where to allocate capital, and how to drive product innovation. Think "RAPID": Who should **r**ecommend a course of action on a key decision? Who must **a**gree to a recommendation before it can move forward? Who will **p**erform the actions needed to implement the decision? Whose **i**nput is needed to determine the proposal's feasibility? Who **d**ecides—brings the decision to closure and commits the organization to implement it?

When you clarify decision roles, you make the *right* choices—swiftly and effectively.

The first of these bottlenecks, *global versus local* decision making, can occur in nearly every major business process and function. Decisions about brand building and product development frequently get snared here, when companies wrestle over how much authority local businesses should have to tailor products for their markets. Marketing is another classic global versus local issue—should local markets have the power to determine pricing and advertising?

The second bottleneck, *center versus business unit* decision making, tends to afflict parent companies and their subsidiaries. Business units are on the front line, close to the customer; the center sees the big picture, sets broad goals, and keeps the organization focused on winning. Where should the decision-making power lie? Should a major capital investment, for example, depend on the approval of the business unit that will own it, or should headquarters make the final call?

Idea in Practice

The RAPID Decision Model

For every strategic decision, assign the following roles and responsibilities:

People Who . . .	Are Responsible For . . .
Recommend	• Making a proposal on a key decision, gathering input, and providing data and analysis to make a sensible choice in a timely fashion • Consulting with input providers—hearing and incorporating their views, and winning their buy-in
Agree	• Negotiating a modified proposal with the recommender if they have concerns about the original proposal • Escalating unresolved issues to the decider if the "A" and "R" can't resolve differences • If necessary, exercising veto power over the recommendation
Perform	• Executing a decision once it's made • Seeing that the decision is implemented promptly and effectively
Input	• Providing relevant facts to the recommender that shed light on the proposal's feasibility and practical implications
Decide	• Serving as the single point of accountability • Bringing the decision to closure by resolving any impasse in the decision-making process • Committing the organization to implementing the decision

Function versus function decision making is perhaps the most common bottleneck. Every manufacturer, for instance, faces a balancing act between product development and marketing during the design of a new product. Who should decide what? Cross-functional decisions too often result in ineffective compromise solutions, which frequently need to be revisited because the right people were not involved at the outset.

Decision-Role Pitfalls

In assigning decision roles:

- Ensure that only one person "has the D." If two or more people think they're in charge of a particular decision, a tug-of-war results.

- Watch for a proliferation of "A's." Too many people with veto power can paralyze recommenders. If many people must agree, you probably haven't pushed decisions down far enough in your organization.

- Avoid assigning too many "I's." When many people give input, at least some of them aren't making meaningful contributions.

The RAPID Model in Action

Example: At British department-store chain John Lewis, company buyers wanted to increase sales and reduce complexity by offering fewer salt and pepper mill models. The company launched the streamlined product set without involving the sales staff. And sales fell. Upon visiting the stores, buyers saw that salespeople (not understanding the strategy behind the recommendation) had halved shelf space to match the reduction in product range, rather than maintaining the same space but stocking more of the products.

To fix the problem, the company "gave buyers the D" on how much space product categories would have. Sales staff "had the A": If space allocations didn't make sense to them, they could force additional negotiations. They also "had the P," implementing product layouts in stores.

Once decision roles were clarified, sales of salt and pepper mills exceeded original levels.

The fourth decision-making bottleneck, *inside versus outside partners,* has become familiar with the rise of outsourcing, joint ventures, strategic alliances, and franchising. In such arrangements, companies need to be absolutely clear about which decisions can be owned by the external partner (usually those about the execution of strategy) and which must continue to be made internally (decisions about the strategy itself). In the case of outsourcing, for instance, brand-name apparel and foot-wear marketers once assumed that overseas suppliers could be responsible for decisions about plant employees' wages and working conditions. Big mistake.

Clearing the Bottlenecks

The most important step in unclogging decision-making bottlenecks is assigning clear roles and responsibilities. Good decision makers recognize which decisions really matter to performance. They think through who should recommend a particular path, who needs to agree, who should have input, who has ultimate responsibility for making the decision, and who is accountable for follow-through. They make the process routine. The result: better coordination and quicker response times.

Companies have devised a number of methods to clarify decision roles and assign responsibilities. We have used an approach called RAPID, which has evolved over the years, to help hundreds of companies develop clear decision-making guidelines. It is, for sure, not a panacea (an indecisive decision maker, for example, can ruin any good system), but it's an important start. The letters in RAPID stand for the primary roles in any decision-making process, although these roles are not performed exactly in this order: recommend, agree, perform, input, and decide—the "D." (See the sidebar "A Decision-Making Primer.")

The people who *recommend* a course of action are responsible for making a proposal or offering alternatives. They need data and analysis to support their recommendations, as well as common sense about what's reasonable, practical, and effective.

The people who *agree* to a recommendation are those who need to sign off on it before it can move forward. If they veto a proposal, they must either work with the recommender to come up with an alternative or elevate the issue to the person with the D. For decision making to function smoothly, only a few people should have such veto power. They may be executives responsible for legal or regulatory compliance or the heads of units whose operations will be significantly affected by the decision.

People with *input* responsibilities are consulted about the recommendation. Their role is to provide the relevant facts that are the basis of any good decision: How practical is the proposal? Can manufacturing accommodate the design change? Where there's dissent or contrasting views, it's important to get these people to the table at the right time. The recommender has no obligation to act on the input he or she receives but is expected to take it into account—particularly since the people who provide input are generally among those who must implement a decision. Consensus is a worthy goal, but as a decision-making standard, it can be an obstacle to action or a recipe for lowest-common-denominator compromise. A more practical objective is to get everyone involved to buy in to the decision.

Eventually, one person will *decide*. The decision maker is the single point of accountability who must bring the decision to closure and commit the organization to act on it. To be strong and effective, the person with the D needs good business judgment, a grasp of the relevant trade-offs, a bias for action, and a keen awareness of the organization that will execute the decision.

The final role in the process involves the people who will *perform* the decision. They see to it that the decision is implemented promptly and effectively. It's a crucial role. Very often, a good decision executed quickly beats a brilliant decision implemented slowly or poorly.

RAPID can be used to help redesign the way an organization works or to target a single bottleneck. Some companies use the approach for the top ten to 20 decisions, or just for the CEO and his or her direct reports. Other companies use it throughout the organization— to improve customer service by clarifying decision roles on the front line, for instance. When people see an effective process for making decisions, they spread the word. For example, after senior managers at a major U.S. retailer used RAPID to sort out a particularly thorny set of corporate decisions, they promptly built the process into their own functional organizations.

To see the process in action, let's look at the way four companies have worked through their decision-making bottlenecks.

A Decision-Making Primer

GOOD DECISION MAKING DEPENDS on assigning clear and specific roles. This sounds simple enough, but many companies struggle to make decisions because lots of people feel accountable—or no one does. RAPID and other tools used to analyze decision making give senior management teams a method for assigning roles and involving the relevant people. The key is to be clear who has input, who gets to decide, and who gets it done.

The five letters in RAPID correspond to the five critical decision-making roles: recommend, agree, perform, input, and decide. As you'll see, the roles are not carried out lockstep in this order—we took some liberties for the sake of creating a useful acronym.

Recommend

People in this role are responsible for making a proposal, gathering input, and providing the right data and analysis to make a sensible decision in a timely fashion. In the course of developing a proposal, recommenders consult with the people who provide input, not just hearing and incorporating their views but also building buy in along the way. Recommenders must have analytical skills, common sense, and organizational smarts.

Agree

Individuals in this role have veto power—yes or no—over the recommendation. Exercising the veto triggers a debate between themselves and the recommenders, which should lead to a modified proposal. If that takes too long, or if the two parties simply can't agree, they can escalate the issue to the person who has the D.

Input

These people are consulted on the decision. Because the people who provide input are typically involved in implementation, recommenders have a

---

Global Versus Local

Every major company today operates in global markets, buying raw materials in one place, shipping them somewhere else, and selling finished products all over the world. Most are trying simultaneously to build local presence and expertise, and to achieve economies of scale. Decision making in this environment is far from straightforward. Frequently, decisions cut across the boundaries between strong interest in taking their advice seriously. No input is binding, but this shouldn't undermine its importance. If the right people are not involved and motivated, the decision is far more likely to falter during execution.

Decide

The person with the D is the formal decision maker. He or she is ultimately accountable for the decision, for better or worse, and has the authority to resolve any impasse in the decision-making process and to commit the organization to action.

Perform

Once a decision is made, a person or group of people will be responsible for executing it. In some instances, the people responsible for implementing a decision are the same people who recommended it.

Writing down the roles and assigning accountability are essential steps, but good decision making also requires the right process. Too many rules can cause the process to collapse under its own weight. The most effective process is grounded in specifics but simple enough to adapt if necessary.

When the process gets slowed down, the problem can often be traced back to one of three trouble spots. First is a lack of clarity about who has the D. If more than one person think they have it for a particular decision, that decision will get caught up in a tug-of-war. The flip side can be equally damaging: No one is accountable for crucial decisions, and the business suffers. Second, a proliferation of people who have veto power can make life tough for recommenders. If a company has too many people in the "agree" role, it usually means that decisions are not pushed down far enough in the organization. Third, if there are a lot of people giving input, it's a signal that at least some of them aren't making a meaningful contribution.

global and local managers, and sometimes across a regional layer in between: What investments will streamline our supply chain? How far should we go in standardizing products or tailoring them for local markets?

The trick in decision making is to avoid becoming either mindlessly global or hopelessly local. If decision-making authority tilts too far toward global executives, local customers' preferences can easily be overlooked, undermining the efficiency and agility of local operations.

But with too much local authority, a company is likely to miss out on crucial economies of scale or opportunities with global clients.

To strike the right balance, a company must recognize its most important sources of value and make sure that decision roles line up with them. This was the challenge facing Martin Broughton, the former CEO and chairman of British American Tobacco, the second-largest tobacco company in the world. In 1993, when Broughton was appointed chief executive, BAT was losing ground to its nearest competitor. Broughton knew that the company needed to take better advantage of its global scale, but decision roles and responsibilities were at odds with this goal. Four geographic operating units ran themselves autonomously, rarely collaborating and sometimes even competing. Achieving consistency across global brands proved difficult, and cost synergies across the operating units were elusive. Industry insiders joked that "there are seven major tobacco companies in the world—and four of them are British American Tobacco." Broughton vowed to change the punch line.

The chief executive envisioned an organization that could take advantage of the opportunities a global business offers—global brands that could compete with established winners such as Altria Group's Marlboro; global purchasing of important raw materials, including tobacco; and more consistency in innovation and customer management. But Broughton didn't want the company to lose its nimbleness and competitive hunger in local markets by shifting too much decision-making power to global executives.

The first step was to clarify roles for the most important decisions. Procurement became a proving ground. Previously, each operating unit had identified its own suppliers and negotiated contracts for all materials. Under Broughton, a global procurement team was set up in headquarters and given authority to choose suppliers and negotiate pricing and quality for global materials, including bulk tobacco and certain types of packaging. Regional procurement teams were now given input into global materials strategies but ultimately had to implement the team's decision. As soon as the global team signed contracts with suppliers, responsibility shifted to the regional teams, who worked out the details of delivery and service with the suppliers in their regions. For materials that did not offer global economies of scale (mentholated filters for the North American market, for example), the regional teams retained their decision-making authority.

As the effort to revamp decision making in procurement gained momentum, the company set out to clarify roles in all its major decisions. The process wasn't easy. A company the size of British American Tobacco has a huge number of moving parts, and developing a practical system for making decisions requires sweating lots of details. What's more, decision-making authority is power, and people are often reluctant to give it up.

It's crucial for the people who will live with the new system to help design it. At BAT, Broughton created working groups led by people earmarked, implicitly or explicitly, for leadership roles in the future. For example, Paul Adams, who ultimately succeeded Broughton as chief executive, was asked to lead the group charged with redesigning decision making for brand and customer management. At the time, Adams was a regional head within one of the operating units. With other senior executives, including some of his own direct reports, Broughton specified that their role was to provide input, not to veto recommendations. Broughton didn't make the common mistake of seeking consensus, which is often an obstacle to action. Instead, he made it clear that the objective was not deciding whether to change the decision-making process but achieving buy in about how to do so as effectively as possible.

The new decision roles provided the foundation the company needed to operate successfully on a global basis while retaining flexibility at the local level. The focus and efficiency of its decision making were reflected in the company's results: After the decision-making overhaul, British American Tobacco experienced nearly ten years of growth well above the levels of its competitors in sales, profits, and market value. The company has gone on to have one of the best-performing stocks on the UK market and has reemerged as a major global player in the tobacco industry.

Center Versus Business Unit

The first rule for making good decisions is to involve the right people at the right level of the organization. For BAT, capturing economies of scale required its global team to appropriate some decision-making powers from regional divisions. For many companies, a similar balancing act takes place between executives at the center and managers in the business units. If too many decisions flow to the center, decision making can grind to a halt. The problem is different but no less critical if the decisions that are elevated to senior executives are the wrong ones.

Companies often grow into this type of problem. In small and midsize organizations, a single management team—sometimes a single leader—effectively handles every major decision. As a company grows and its operations become more complex, however, senior executives can no longer master the details required to make decisions in every business.

A change in management style, often triggered by the arrival of a new CEO, can create similar tensions. At a large British retailer, for example, the senior team was accustomed to the founder making all critical decisions. When his successor began seeking consensus on important issues, the team was suddenly unsure of its role, and many decisions stalled. It's a common scenario, yet most management teams and boards of directors don't specify how decision-making authority should change as the company does.

A growth opportunity highlighted that issue for Wyeth (then known as American Home Products) in late 2000. Through organic growth, acquisitions, and partnerships, Wyeth's pharmaceutical division had developed three sizable businesses: biotech, vaccines, and traditional pharmaceutical products. Even though each business had its own market dynamics, operating requirements, and research focus, most important decisions were pushed up to one group of senior executives. "We were using generalists across all issues," said Joseph M. Mahady, president of North American and global businesses for Wyeth Pharmaceuticals. "It was a signal that we weren't getting our best decision making."

The problem crystallized for Wyeth when managers in the biotech business saw a vital—but perishable—opportunity to establish a leading position with Enbrel, a promising rheumatoid arthritis drug. Competitors were working on the same class of drug, so Wyeth needed to move quickly. This meant expanding production capacity by building a new plant, which would be located at the Grange Castle Business Park in Dublin, Ireland.

The decision, by any standard, was a complex one. Once approved by regulators, the facility would be the biggest biotech plant in the world—and the largest capital investment Wyeth had ever undertaken. Yet peak demand for the drug was not easy to determine. What's more, Wyeth planned to market Enbrel in partnership with Immunex (now a part of Amgen). In its deliberations about the plant, therefore, Wyeth needed to factor in the requirements of building up its technical expertise, technology transfer issues, and an uncertain competitive environment.

Input on the decision filtered up slowly through a gauze of overlapping committees, leaving senior executives hungry for a more detailed grasp of the issues. Given the narrow window of opportunity, Wyeth acted quickly, moving from a first look at the Grange Castle project to implementation in six months. But in the midst of this process, Wyeth Pharmaceuticals' executives saw the larger issue: The company needed a system that would push more decisions down to the business units, where operational knowledge was greatest, and elevate the decisions that required the senior team's input, such as marketing strategy and manufacturing capacity.

In short order, Wyeth gave authority for many decisions to business unit managers, leaving senior executives with veto power over some of the more sensitive issues related to Grange Castle. But after that investment decision was made, the D for many subsequent decisions about the Enbrel business lay with Cavan Redmond, the executive vice president and general manager of Wyeth's biotech division, and his new management team. Redmond gathered input from managers in biotech manufacturing, marketing, forecasting, finance, and R&D, and quickly set up the complex schedules needed to collaborate with Immunex. Responsibility for execution rested firmly with the business unit, as always. But now Redmond, supported by his team, also had authority to make important decisions.

Grange Castle is paying off so far. Enbrel is among the leading brands for rheumatoid arthritis, with sales of $1.7 billion through the first half of 2005. And Wyeth's metabolism for making decisions has increased. Recently, when the U.S. Food and Drug Administration granted priority review status to another new drug, Tygacil, because of the antibiotic's efficacy against drug-resistant infections, Wyeth displayed its new reflexes. To keep Tygacil on a fast track, the company had to orchestrate a host of critical steps—refining the process technology, lining up supplies, ensuring quality control, allocating manufacturing capacity. The vital decisions were made one or two levels down in the biotech organization, where the expertise resided. "Instead of debating whether you can move your product into my shop, we had the decision systems in place to run it up and down the business units and move ahead rapidly with Tygacil," said Mahady. The drug was approved by the FDA in June 2005 and moved into volume production a mere three days later.

Function Versus Function

Decisions that cut across functions are some of the most important a company faces. Indeed, cross-functional collaboration has become an axiom of business, essential for arriving at the best answers for the company and its customers. But fluid decision making across functional teams remains a constant challenge, even for companies known for doing it well, like Toyota and Dell. For instance, a team that thinks it's more efficient to make a decision without consulting other functions may wind up missing out on relevant input or being overruled by another team that believes—rightly or wrongly—it should have been included in the process. Many of the most important cross-functional decisions are, by their very nature, the most difficult to orchestrate, and that can string out the process and lead to sparring between fiefdoms and costly indecision.

The theme here is a lack of clarity about who has the D. For example, at a global auto manufacturer that was missing its milestones

A Recipe for a Decision-Making Bottleneck

AT ONE AUTOMAKER WE STUDIED, marketers and product developers were confused about who was responsible for making decisions about new models.

When we asked, "Who has the right to decide which features will be standard?"

64% of product developers said, "We do."

83% of marketers said, "We do."

When we asked, "Who has the right to decide which colors will be offered?"

77% of product developers said, "We do."

61% of marketers said, "We do."

Not surprisingly, the new models were delayed.

for rolling out new models—and was paying the price in falling sales—it turned out that marketers and product developers were confused about which function was responsible for making decisions about standard features and color ranges for new models. When we asked the marketing team who had the D about which features should be standard, 83% said the marketers did. When we posed the same question to product developers, 64% said the responsibility rested with them. (See "A Recipe for a Decision-Making Bottleneck.")

The practical difficulty of connecting functions through smooth decision making crops up frequently at retailers. John Lewis, the leading department store chain in the United Kingdom, might reasonably expect to overcome this sort of challenge more readily than other retailers. Spedan Lewis, who built the business in the early twentieth century, was a pioneer in employee ownership. A strong connection between managers and employees permeated every aspect of the store's operations and remained vital to the company as it grew into the largest employee-owned business in the United Kingdom, with 59,600 employees and more than £5 billion in revenues in 2004.

Even at John Lewis, however, with its heritage of cooperation and teamwork, cross-functional decision making can be hard to sustain. Take salt and pepper mills, for instance. John Lewis, which prides itself on having great selection, stocked nearly 50 SKUs of salt and pepper mills, while most competitors stocked around 20. The company's buyers saw an opportunity to increase sales and reduce complexity by offering a smaller number of popular and well-chosen products in each price point and style.

When John Lewis launched the new range, sales fell. This made no sense to the buyers until they visited the stores and saw how the merchandise was displayed. The buyers had made their decision without fully involving the sales staff, who therefore did not understand the strategy behind the new selection. As a result, the sellers had cut shelf space in half to match the reduction in range, rather than devoting the same amount of shelf space to stocking more of each product.

To fix the communication problem, John Lewis needed to clarify decision roles. The buyers were given the D on how much space to allocate to each product category. If the space allocation didn't make sense to the sales staff, however, they had the authority to raise their concerns and force a new round of negotiations. They also had responsibility for implementing product layouts in the stores. When the communication was sorted out and shelf space was restored, sales of the salt and pepper mills climbed well above original levels.

Crafting a decision-making process that connected the buying and selling functions for salt and pepper mills was relatively easy; rolling it out across the entire business was more challenging. Salt and pepper mills are just one of several hundred product categories for John Lewis. This element of scale is one reason why cross-functional bottlenecks are not easy to unclog. Different functions have different incentives and goals, which are often in conflict. When it comes down to a struggle between two functions, there may be good reasons to locate the D in either place—buying or selling, marketing or product development.

Here, as elsewhere, someone needs to think objectively about where value is created and assign decision roles accordingly. Eliminating cross-functional bottlenecks actually has less to do with shifting decision-making responsibilities between departments and more to do with ensuring that the people with relevant information are allowed to share it. The decision maker is important, of course, but more important is designing a system that aligns decision making and makes it routine.

Inside Versus Outside Partners

Decision making within an organization is hard enough. Trying to make decisions between separate organizations on different continents adds layers of complexity that can scuttle the best strategy. Companies that outsource capabilities in pursuit of cost and quality advantages face this very challenge. Which decisions should be made internally? Which can be delegated to outsourcing partners?

These questions are also relevant for strategic partners—a global bank working with an IT contractor on a systems development project, for example, or a media company that acquires content from a studio—and for companies conducting part of their business through franchisees. There is no right answer to who should have the power to decide what. But the wrong approach is to assume that contractual arrangements can provide the answer.

An outdoor-equipment company based in the United States discovered this recently when it decided to scale up production of gas patio heaters for the lower end of the market. The company had some success manufacturing high-end products in China. But with the advent of superdiscounters like Wal-Mart, Target, and Home Depot, the company realized it needed to move more of its production overseas to feed these retailers with lower-cost offerings. The timetable left little margin for error: The company started tooling up factories in April and June of 2004, hoping to be ready for the Christmas season.

Right away, there were problems. Although the Chinese manufacturing partners understood costs, they had little idea what American consumers wanted. When expensive designs arrived from the head office in the United States, Chinese plant managers made compromises to meet contracted cost targets. They used a lower grade material, which discolored. They placed the power switch in a spot that was inconvenient for the user but easier to build. Instead

The Decision-Driven Organization

THE DEFINING CHARACTERISTIC of high-performing organizations is their ability to make good decisions and to make them happen quickly. The companies that succeed tend to follow a few clear principles.

Some decisions matter more than others.

The decisions that are crucial to building value in the business are the ones that matter most. Some of them will be the big strategic decisions, but just as important are the critical operating decisions that drive the business day to day and are vital to effective execution.

Action is the goal.

Good decision making doesn't end with a decision; it ends with implementation. The objective shouldn't be consensus, which often becomes an obstacle to action, but buy in.

Ambiguity is the enemy.

Clear accountability is essential: Who contributes input, who makes the decision, and who carries it out? Without clarity, gridlock and delay are the most likely outcomes. Clarity doesn't necessarily mean concentrating authority in a few people; it means defining who has responsibility to make decisions, who has input, and who is charged with putting them into action.

Speed and adaptability are crucial.

A company that makes good decisions quickly has a higher metabolism, which allows it to act on opportunities and overcome obstacles. The best decision makers create an environment where people can come together quickly and efficiently to make the most important decisions.

Decision roles trump the organizational chart.

No decision-making structure will be perfect for every decision. The key is to involve the right people at the right level in the right part of the organization at the right time.

A well-aligned organization reinforces roles.

Clear decision roles are critical, but they are not enough. If an organization does not reinforce the right approach to decision making through its measures and incentives, information flows, and culture, the behavior won't become routine.

Practicing beats preaching.

Involve the people who will live with the new decision roles in designing them. The very process of thinking about new decision behaviors motivates people to adopt them.

A Decision Diagnostic

CONSIDER THE LAST THREE MEANINGFUL decisions you've been involved in and ask yourself the following questions.

1. Were the decisions right?

2. Were they made with appropriate speed?

3. Were they executed well?

4. Were the right people involved, in the right way?

5. Was it clear for each decision

   - who would recommend a solution?

   - who would provide input?

   - who had the final say?

   - who would be responsible for following through?

6. Were the decision roles, process, and time frame respected?

7. Were the decisions based on appropriate facts?

8. To the extent that there were divergent facts or opinions, was it clear who had the D?

9. Were the decision makers at the appropriate level in the company?

10. Did the organization's measures and incentives encourage the people involved to make the right decisions?

of making certain parts from a single casting, they welded materials together, which looked terrible.

To fix these problems, the U.S. executives had to draw clear lines around which decisions should be made on which side of the ocean. The company broke down the design and manufacturing process into five steps and analyzed how decisions were made at each step. The company was also much more explicit about what the manufacturing specs would include and what the manufacturer was expected to do with them. The objective was not simply to clarify decision roles but to make sure those roles corresponded directly to the sources of value in the business. If a decision would affect the look and feel of the finished product, headquarters would have to sign off on it.

But if a decision would not affect the customer's experience, it could be made in China. If, for example, Chinese engineers found a less expensive material that didn't compromise the product's look, feel, and functionality, they could make that change on their own.

To help with the transition to this system, the company put a team of engineers on-site in China to ensure a smooth handoff of the specs and to make decisions on issues that would become complex and time-consuming if elevated to the home office. Marketing executives in the home office insisted that it should take a customer ten minutes and no more than six steps to assemble the product at home. The company's engineers in China, along with the Chinese manufacturing team, had input into this assembly requirement and were responsible for execution. But the D resided with headquarters, and the requirement became a major design factor. Decisions about logistics, however, became the province of the engineering team in China: It would figure out how to package the heaters so that one-third more boxes would fit into a container, which reduced shipping costs substantially.

If managers suddenly realize that they're spending less time sitting through meetings wondering why they are there, that's an early signal that companies have become better at making decisions. When meetings start with a common understanding about who is responsible for providing valuable input and who has the D, an organization's decision-making metabolism will get a boost.

No single lever turns a decision-challenged organization into a decision-driven one, of course, and no blueprint can provide for all the contingencies and business shifts a company is bound to encounter. The most successful companies use simple tools that help them recognize potential bottlenecks and think through decision roles and responsibilities with each change in the business environment. That's difficult to do—and even more difficult for competitors to copy. But by taking some very practical steps, any company can become more effective, beginning with its next decision.

Originally published in January 2006. Reprint R0601D.

In Praise of the Incomplete Leader

by Deborah Ancona, Thomas W. Malone, Wanda J. Orlikowski, and Peter M. Senge

WE'VE COME TO EXPECT A LOT OF OUR LEADERS. Top executives, the thinking goes, should have the intellectual capacity to make sense of unfathomably complex issues, the imaginative powers to paint a vision of the future that generates everyone's enthusiasm, the operational know-how to translate strategy into concrete plans, and the interpersonal skills to foster commitment to undertakings that could cost people's jobs should they fail. Unfortunately, no single person can possibly live up to those standards.

It's time to end the myth of the complete leader: the flawless person at the top who's got it all figured out. In fact, the sooner leaders stop trying to be all things to all people, the better off their organizations will be. In today's world, the executive's job is no longer to command and control but to cultivate and coordinate the actions of others at all levels of the organization. Only when leaders come to see themselves as incomplete—as having both strengths and weaknesses—will they be able to make up for their missing skills by relying on others.

Corporations have been becoming less hierarchical and more collaborative for decades, of course, as globalization and the growing importance of knowledge work have required that responsibility and initiative be distributed more widely. Moreover, it is now possible for large groups of people to coordinate their actions, not just by bringing lots of information to a few centralized places but also by bringing lots of information to lots of places through ever-growing networks within and beyond the firm. The sheer complexity and ambiguity of problems is humbling. More and more decisions are made in the context of global markets and rapidly—sometimes radically—changing financial, social, political, technological, and environmental forces. Stakeholders such as activists, regulators, and employees all have claims on organizations.

No one person could possibly stay on top of everything. But the myth of the complete leader (and the attendant fear of appearing incompetent) makes many executives try to do just that, exhausting themselves and damaging their organizations in the process. The incomplete leader, by contrast, knows when to let go: when to let those who know the local market do the advertising plan or when to let the engineering team run with its idea of what the customer needs. The incomplete leader also knows that leadership exists throughout the organizational hierarchy—wherever expertise, vision, new ideas, and commitment are found.

We've worked with hundreds of people who have struggled under the weight of the myth of the complete leader. Over the past six years, our work at the MIT Leadership Center has included studying leadership in many organizations and teaching the topic to senior executives, middle managers, and MBA students. In our practice-based programs, we have analyzed numerous accounts of organizational change and watched leaders struggle to meld top-down strategic initiatives with vibrant ideas from the rest of the organization.

All this work has led us to develop a model of distributed leadership. This framework, which synthesizes our own research with ideas from other leadership scholars, views leadership as a set of four capabilities: *sensemaking* (understanding the context in which a company and its people operate), *relating* (building relationships within and across organizations), *visioning* (creating a compelling picture of the future), and *inventing* (developing new ways to achieve the vision).

Idea in Brief

Have you ever feigned confidence to superiors or reports? Hidden the fact you were confused by the latest business results or blind-sided by a competitor's move? If so, you've bought into the **myth of the complete leader:** the flawless being at the top who's got it all figured out.

It's an alluring myth. But in today's world of increasingly complex problems, no human being can meet this standard. Leaders who try only exhaust themselves, endangering their organizations.

Ancona and her coauthors suggest a better way to lead: Accept that you're human, with strengths and weaknesses. Understand the four leadership capabilities all organizations need:

- Sensemaking—interpreting developments in the business environment

- Relating—building trusting relationships

- Visioning—communicating a compelling image of the future

- Inventing—coming up with new ways of doing things

Then find and work with others who can provide the capabilities you're missing.

Take this approach, and you promote leadership throughout your organization, unleashing the expertise, vision, and new ideas your company needs to excel.

While somewhat simplified, these capabilities span the intellectual and interpersonal, the rational and intuitive, and the conceptual and creative capacities required in today's business environment. Rarely, if ever, will someone be equally skilled in all four domains. Thus, incomplete leaders differ from incompetent leaders in that they understand what they're good at and what they're not and have good judgment about how they can work with others to build on their strengths and offset their limitations.

Sometimes, leaders need to further develop the capabilities they are weakest in. The exhibits throughout this article provide some suggestions for when and how to do that. Other times, however, it's more important for leaders to find and work with others to compensate for their weaknesses. Teams and organizations—not just individuals—can use this framework to diagnose their strengths and weaknesses and find ways to balance their skill sets.

Idea in Practice

Incomplete leaders find people throughout their company who can complement their strengths and offset their weaknesses. To do this, understand the four leadership capabilities organizations need. Then diagnose your strength in each:

Capability	What it means	Example	Look for help in this capability if you ...
Sensemaking	Constantly understanding changes in the business environment and interpreting their ramifications for your industry and company	A CEO asks, "How will new technologies reshape our industry?" "How does globalization of labor markets affect our recruitment strategy?"	• Feel strongly that you're always right. • Frequently get blindsided by changes in your company or industry. • Feel resentful when things change.
Relating	Building trusting relationships, balancing advocacy (explaining your viewpoints) with inquiry (listening to understand others' viewpoints), and cultivating networks of supportive confidants	Former Southwest Airlines CEO Herb Kelleher excels at building trusting relationships. He wasn't afraid to tell employees he loved them, and reinforced those emotional bonds with equitable compensation and profit sharing.	• Blame others for failed projects. • Feel others are constantly letting you down or that they can't be trusted. • Frequently experience unpleasant, frustrating, or argumentative interactions with others.

Sensemaking

The term "sensemaking" was coined by organizational psychologist Karl Weick, and it means just what it sounds like: making sense of the world around us. Leaders are constantly trying to understand the contexts they are operating in. How will new technologies reshape the industry? How will changing cultural expectations shift the role

Visioning	Creating credible and compelling images of a desired future that people in the organization want to create together	eBay founder Pierre Omidyar envisioned a new way of doing large-scale retailing: an online community where users took responsibility for what happened and had equal access to information.	• Often wonder, "Why are we doing this?" or "Does it really matter?" • Can't remember the last time you felt excited about your work. • Feel you're lacking sense of larger purpose.
Inventing	Creating new ways of approaching tasks or overcoming seemingly insurmountable problems to turn visions into reality	eBay CEO Meg Whitman helped bring Omidyar's vision of online retailing to life by inventing ways to deal with security, vendor reliability, and product diversification.	• Have difficulty relating the company's vision to what you're doing today. • Notice gaps between your firm's aspirations and the way work is organized. • Find that things tend to revert to business as usual.

of business in society? How does the globalization of labor markets affect recruitment and expansion plans?

Weick likened the process of sensemaking to cartography. What we map depends on where we look, what factors we choose to focus on, and what aspects of the terrain we decide to represent. Since these choices will shape the kind of map we produce, there is no perfect map of a terrain. Therefore, making sense is more than an

Engage in sensemaking

1. Get data from multiple sources: customers, suppliers, employees, competitors, other departments, and investors.

2. Involve others in your sensemaking. Say what you think you are seeing, and check with people who have different perspectives from yours.

3. Use early observations to shape small experiments in order to test your conclusions. Look for new ways to articulate alternatives and better ways to understand options.

4. Do not simply apply existing frameworks but instead be open to new possibilities. Try not to describe the world in stereotypical ways, such as good guys and bad guys, victims and oppressors, or marketers and engineers.

act of analysis; it's an act of creativity. (See the exhibit "Engage in sensemaking.")

The key for leaders is to determine what would be a useful map given their particular goals and then to draw one that adequately represents the situation the organization is facing at that moment. Executives who are strong in this capability know how to quickly capture the complexities of their environment and explain them to others in simple terms. This helps ensure that everyone is working from the same map, which makes it far easier to discuss and plan for the journey ahead. Leaders need to have the courage to present a map that highlights features they believe to be critical, even if their map doesn't conform to the dominant perspective.

When John Reed was CEO of Citibank, the company found itself in a real estate crisis. At the time, common wisdom said that Citibank would need to take a $2 billion write-off, but Reed wasn't sure. He wanted a better understanding of the situation, so to map the problem, he met with federal regulators as well as his managers, the board, potential investors, economists, and real estate experts. He kept asking, "What am I missing here?" After those meetings, he had a much stronger grasp of the problem, and he recalibrated the write-off to $5 billion—which turned out to be a far more accurate estimate. Later, three quarters into the bank's eight-quarter program to deal with the crisis, Reed realized that progress had stopped. He began talking to other CEOs known for their change management skills. This informal benchmarking process led him to devise an organizational redesign.

Throughout the crisis, real estate valuations, investors' requirements, board demands, and management team expectations were all changing and constantly needed to be reassessed. Good leaders understand that sensemaking is a continuous process; they let the map emerge from a melding of observations, data, experiences, conversations, and analyses. In healthy organizations, this sort of sensemaking goes on all the time. People have ongoing dialogues about their interpretations of markets and organizational realities.

At IDEO, a product design firm, sensemaking is step one for all design teams. According to founder David Kelley, team members must act as anthropologists studying an alien culture to understand the potential product from all points of view. When brainstorming a new design, IDEO's teams consider multiple perspectives—that is, they build multiple maps to inform their creative process. One IDEO team was charged with creating a new design for an emergency room. To better understand the experience of a key stakeholder—the patient—team members attached a camera to a patient's head and captured his experience in the ER. The result: nearly ten full hours of film of the ceiling. The sensemaking provoked by this perspective led to a redesign of the ceiling that made it more aesthetically pleasing and able to display important information for patients.

Relating

Many executives who attempt to foster trust, optimism, and consensus often reap anger, cynicism, and conflict instead. That's because they have difficulty relating to others, especially those who don't make sense of the world the way they do. Traditional images of leadership didn't assign much value to relating. Flawless leaders shouldn't need to seek counsel from anyone outside their tight inner circle, the thinking went, and they were expected to issue edicts rather than connect on an emotional level. Times have changed, of course, and in this era of networks, being able to build trusting relationships is a requirement of effective leadership.

Three key ways to do this are *inquiring, advocating,* and *connecting.* The concepts of inquiring and advocating stem from the work of organizational development specialists Chris Argyris and Don Schon. Inquiring means listening with the intention of genuinely understanding the thoughts and feelings of the speaker. Here, the listener suspends judgment and tries to comprehend how and why the speaker has moved from the data of his or her experiences to particular interpretations and conclusions.

Advocating, as the term implies, means explaining one's own point of view. It is the flip side of inquiring, and it's how leaders make clear to others how they reached their interpretations and conclusions. Good leaders distinguish their observations from their opinions and judgments and explain their reasoning without aggression or defensiveness. People with strong relating skills are typically those who've found a healthy balance between inquiring and advocating: They actively try to understand others' views but are able to stand up for their own. (See the exhibit "Build relationships.")

We've seen countless relationships undermined because people disproportionately emphasized advocating over inquiring. Even though managers pay lip service to the importance of mutual understanding and shared commitment to a course of action, often their real focus is on winning the argument rather than strengthening the connection. Worse, in many organizations, the imbalance goes so far that having one's point of view prevail is what is understood as leadership.

Build relationships

1. Spend time trying to understand others' perspectives, listening with an open mind and without judgment.

2. Encourage others to voice their opinions. What do they care about? How do they interpret what's going on? Why?

3. Before expressing your ideas, try to anticipate how others will react to them and how you might best explain them.

4. When expressing your ideas, don't just give a bottom line; explain your reasoning process.

5. Assess the strengths of your current connections: How well do you relate to others when receiving advice? When giving advice? When thinking through difficult problems? When asking for help?

Effective relating does not mean avoiding interpersonal conflict altogether. Argyris and Schon found that "maintaining a smooth surface" of conviviality and apparent agreement is one of the most common defensive routines that limits team effectiveness. Balancing inquiring and advocating is ultimately about showing respect, challenging opinions, asking tough questions, and taking a stand.

Consider Twynstra Gudde (TG), one of the largest independent consulting companies in the Netherlands. A few years ago, it replaced the role of CEO with a team of four managing directors who share leadership responsibilities. Given this unique structure, it's vital that these directors effectively relate to one another. They've adopted simple rules, such as a requirement that each leader give his opinion on every issue, majority-rules voting, and veto power for each director.

Clearly, for TG's senior team model to work, members must be skilled at engaging in dialogue together. They continually practice both inquiring and advocating, and because each director can veto a decision, each must thoroughly explain his reasoning to convince the others' that his perspective has merit. It's not easy to reach this level of mutual respect and trust, but over time, the team members' willingness to create honest connections with one another has paid off handsomely. Although they don't always reach consensus, they are able to settle on a course of action. Since this new form of leadership was introduced, TG has thrived: The company's profits have doubled, and employee satisfaction levels have improved. What's more, TG's leadership structure has served as a model for cooperation throughout the organization as well as in the firm's relations with its clients.

The third aspect of relating, connecting, involves cultivating a network of confidants who can help a leader accomplish a wide range of goals. Leaders who are strong in this capability have many people they can turn to who can help them think through difficult problems or support them in their initiatives. They understand that the time spent building and maintaining these connections is time spent investing in their leadership skills. Because no one person can possibly have all the answers, or indeed, know all the right questions to ask, it's crucial that leaders be able to tap into a network of people who can fill in the gaps.

Visioning

Sensemaking and relating can be called the enabling capabilities of leadership. They help set the conditions that motivate and sustain change. The next two leadership capabilities—what we call "visioning" and inventing—are creative and action oriented: They produce the focus and energy needed to make change happen.

Visioning involves creating compelling images of the future. While sensemaking charts a map of what is, visioning produces a map of what could be and, more important, what a leader wants the future to be. It consists of far more than pinning a vision statement to the wall. Indeed, a shared vision is not a static thing—it's an ongoing process. Like sensemaking, visioning is dynamic and collaborative, a process of articulating what the members of an organization want to create together.

Fundamentally, visioning gives people a sense of meaning in their work. Leaders who are skilled in this capability are able to get people excited about their view of the future while inviting others to help crystallize that image. (See the exhibit "Create a vision.") If they realize other people aren't joining in or buying into the vision, they don't just turn up the volume; they engage in a dialogue about the reality they hope to produce. They use stories and metaphors to paint a vivid picture of what the vision will accomplish, even if they don't have a comprehensive plan for getting there. They know that if the vision is credible and compelling enough, others will generate ideas to advance it.

In South Africa in the early 1990s, a joke was making the rounds: Given the country's daunting challenges, people had two options, one practical and the other miraculous. The practical option was for everyone to pray for a band of angels to come down from heaven and fix things. The miraculous option was for people to talk with one another until they could find a way forward. In F.W. de Klerk's famous speech in 1990—his first after assuming leadership—he called for a nonracist South Africa and suggested that negotiation was the only way to achieve a peaceful transition. That speech sparked a set of changes that led to Nelson Mandela's release from

Create a vision

1. Practice creating a vision in many arenas, including your work life, your home life, and in community groups. Ask yourself, "What do I want to create?"

2. Develop a vision about something that inspires you. Your enthusiasm will motivate you and others. Listen to what they find exciting and important.

3. Expect that not all people will share your passion. Be prepared to explain why people should care about your vision and what can be achieved through it. If people don't get it, don't just turn up the volume. Try to construct a shared vision.

4. Don't worry if you don't know how to accomplish the vision. If it is compelling and credible, other people will discover all sorts of ways to make it real—ways you never could have imagined on your own.

5. Use images, metaphors, and stories to convey complex situations that will enable others to act.

Robben Island prison and the return to the country of previously banned political leaders.

Few of South Africa's leaders agreed on much of anything regarding the country's future. It seemed like a long shot, at best, that a scenario-planning process convened by a black professor from the University of the Western Cape and facilitated by a white Canadian from Royal Dutch Shell would be able to bring about any sort of change. But they, together with members of the African National Congress (ANC), the radical Pan Africanist Congress (PAC), and the white business community, were charged with forging a new path for South Africa.

When the team members first met, they focused on collective sensemaking. Their discussions then evolved into a yearlong visioning process. In his book, *Solving Tough Problems,* Adam Kahane, the facilitator, says the group started by telling stories of "left-wing revolution, right-wing revolts, and free market utopias." Eventually, the leadership team drafted a set of scenarios that described the many paths toward disaster and the one toward sustainable development.

They used metaphors and clear imagery to convey the various paths in language that was easy to understand. One negative scenario, for instance, was dubbed "Ostrich": A nonrepresentative white government sticks its head in the sand, trying to avoid a negotiated settlement with the black majority. Another negative scenario was labeled "Icarus": A constitutionally unconstrained black government comes to power with noble intentions and embarks on a huge, unsustainable public-spending spree that crashes the economy. This scenario contradicted the popular belief that the country was rich and could simply redistribute wealth from whites to blacks. The Icarus scenario set the stage for a fundamental (and controversial) shift in economic thinking in the ANC and other left-wing parties—a shift that led the ANC government to "strict and consistent fiscal discipline," according to Kahane.

The group's one positive scenario involved the government adopting a set of sustainable policies that would put the country on a path of inclusive growth to successfully rebuild the economy and establish democracy. This option was called "Flamingo," invoking the image of a flock of beautiful birds all taking flight together.

This process of visioning unearthed an extraordinary collective sense of possibility in South Africa. Instead of talking about what other people should do to advance some agenda, the leaders spoke about what they could do to create a better future for everyone. They didn't have an exact implementation plan at the ready, but by creating a credible vision, they paved the way for others to join in and help make their vision a reality.

Leaders who excel in visioning walk the walk; they work to embody the core values and ideas contained in the vision. Darcy Winslow, Nike's global director for women's footwear, is a good example. A 14-year veteran at Nike, Winslow previously held the position of general manager of sustainable business opportunities at the shoe and apparel giant. Her work in that role reflected her own core values, including her passion for the environment. "We had come to see that our customers' health and our own ability to compete were inseparable from the health of the environment," she says. So she initiated the concept of ecologically intelligent product design. Winslow's team worked at determining the chemical composition and environmental effects of every material and process Nike used. They visited factories in China and collected samples of rubber, leather, nylon, polyester, and foams to determine their chemical makeup. This led Winslow and her team to develop a list of "positive" materials—those that weren't harmful to the environment—that they hoped to use in more Nike products. "Environmental sustainability" was no longer just an abstract term on a vision statement; the team now felt a mandate to realize the vision.

Inventing

Even the most compelling vision will lose its power if it floats, unconnected, above the everyday reality of organizational life. To transform a vision of the future into a present-day reality, leaders need to devise processes that will give it life. This inventing is what moves a business from the abstract world of ideas to the concrete world of implementation. In fact, inventing is similar to execution, but the label "inventing" emphasizes that this process often requires creativity to help people figure out new ways of working together.

To realize a new vision, people usually can't keep doing the same things they've been doing. They need to conceive, design, and put into practice new ways of interacting and organizing. Some of the most famous examples of large-scale organizational innovation come from the automotive industry: Henry Ford's conception of the assembly-line factory and Toyota's famed integrated production system.

More recently, Pierre Omidyar, the founder of eBay, invented through his company a new way of doing large-scale retailing. His vision was of an online community where users would take responsibility for what happened. In a 2001 BusinessWeek Online interview, Omidyar explained, "I had the idea that I wanted to create an efficient market and a level playing field where everyone had equal access to information. I wanted to give the power of the market back to individuals, not just large corporations. That was the driving motivation for creating eBay at the start."

Consequently, eBay outsources most of the functions of traditional retailing—purchasing, order fulfillment, and customer service, for example—to independent sellers worldwide. The company estimates that more than 430,000 people make their primary living from selling wares on eBay. If those individuals were all employees of eBay, it would be the second largest private employer in the United States after Wal-Mart.

The people who work through eBay are essentially independent store owners, and, as such, they have a huge amount of autonomy in how they do their work. They decide what to sell, when to sell it, how to price, and how to advertise. Coupled with this individual freedom is global scale. eBay's infrastructure enables them to sell their goods all over the world. What makes eBay's inventing so radical is that it represents a new relationship between an organization and its parts. Unlike typical outsourcing, eBay doesn't pay its retailers—they pay the company.

Inventing doesn't have to occur on such a grand scale. It happens every time a person creates a way of approaching a task or figures out how to overcome a previously insurmountable obstacle. In their book *Car Launch,* George Roth and Art Kleiner describe a highly successful product development team in the automobile industry that struggled with completing its designs on time. Much of the source of the problem, the team members concluded, came from the stovepipe organizational structure found in the product development division. Even though they were a "colocated" team dedicated to designing a common new car, members were divided by their different technical expertise, experience, jargon, and norms of working.

When the team invented a mechanical prototyping device that complemented its computer-aided design tools, the group members found that it facilitated a whole new way of collaborating. Multiple groups within the team could quickly create physical mock-ups of design ideas to be tested by the various engineers from different specialties in the team. The group called the device "the harmony buck," because it helped people break out of their comfortable engineering specialties and solve interdependent design problems together. Development of a "full body" physical mock-up of the new car allowed engineers to hang around the prototype, providing a central focal point for their interactions. It enabled them to more easily identify and raise cross-functional issues, and it facilitated mutual problem solving and coordination.

Cultivate inventiveness

1. Don't assume that the way things have always been done is the best way to do them.

2. When a new task or change effort emerges, encourage creative ways of getting it done.

3. Experiment with different ways of organizing work. Find alternative methods for grouping and linking people.

4. When working to understand your current environment, ask yourself, "What other options are possible?"

In sum, leaders must be able to succeed at inventing, and this requires both attention to detail and creativity. (See the exhibit "Cultivate inventiveness.")

Balancing the Four Capabilities

Sensemaking, relating, visioning, and inventing are interdependent. Without sensemaking, there's no common view of reality from which to start. Without relating, people work in isolation or, worse, strive toward different aims. Without visioning, there's no shared direction. And without inventing, a vision remains illusory. No one leader, however, will excel at all four capabilities in equal measure.

Typically, leaders are strong in one or two capabilities. Intel chairman Andy Grove is the quintessential sensemaker, for instance, with a gift for recognizing strategic inflection points that can be exploited for competitive advantage. Herb Kelleher, the former CEO of Southwest Airlines, excels at relating. He remarked in the journal *Leader to Leader* that "We are not afraid to talk to our people with emotion. We're not afraid to tell them, 'We love you.' Because we do." With this emotional connection comes equitable compensation and profit sharing.

Apple CEO Steve Jobs is a visionary whose ambitious dreams and persuasiveness have catalyzed remarkable successes for Apple, Next, and Pixar. Meg Whitman, the CEO of eBay, helped bring Pierre Omidyar's vision of online retailing to life by inventing ways to deal with security, vendor reliability, and product diversification.

Once leaders diagnose their own capabilities, identifying their unique set of strengths and weaknesses, they must search for

Examining Your Leadership Capabilities

FEW PEOPLE WAKE UP in the morning and say, "I'm a poor sensemaker" or "I just can't relate to others." They tend to experience their own weaknesses more as chronic or inexplicable failures in the organization or in those around them. The following descriptions will help you recognize opportunities to develop your leadership capabilities and identify openings for working with others.

Signs of Weak Sensemaking

1. You feel strongly that you are usually right and others are often wrong.

2. You feel your views describe reality correctly, but others' views do not.

3. You find you are often blindsided by changes in your organization or industry.

4. When things change, you typically feel resentful. (That's not the way it should be!)

Signs of Weak Relating

1. You blame others for failed projects.

2. You feel others are constantly letting you down or failing to live up to your expectations.

others who can provide the things they're missing. (See the sidebar "Examining Your Leadership Capabilities.") Leaders who choose only people who mirror themselves are likely to find their organizations tilting in one direction, missing one or more essential capabilities needed to survive in a changing, complex world. That's why it's important to examine the whole organization to make sure it is appropriately balanced as well. It's the leader's responsibility to create an environment that lets people complement one another's strengths and offset one another's weaknesses. In this way, leadership is distributed across multiple people throughout the organization.

Years ago, one of us attended a three-day meeting on leadership with 15 top managers from different companies. At the close of it,

3. You find that many of your interactions at work are unpleasant, frustrating, or argumentative.

4. You find many of the people you work with untrustworthy.

Signs of Weak Visioning

1. You feel your work involves managing an endless series of crises.

2. You feel like you're bouncing from pillar to post with no sense of larger purpose.

3. You often wonder, "Why are we doing this?" or "Does it really matter?"

4. You can't remember the last time you talked to your family or a friend with excitement about your work.

Signs of Weak Inventing

1. Your organization's vision seems abstract to you.

2. You have difficulty relating your company's vision to what you are doing today.

3. You notice dysfunctional gaps between your organization's aspirations and the way work is organized.

4. You find that things tend to revert to business as usual.

---

participants were asked to reflect on their experience as leaders. One executive, responsible for more than 50,000 people in his division of a manufacturing corporation, drew two pictures on a flip chart. The image on the left was what he projected to the outside world: It was a large, intimidating face holding up a huge fist. The image on the right represented how he saw himself: a small face with wide eyes, hair standing on end, and an expression of sheer terror.

We believe that most leaders experience that profound dichotomy every day, and it's a heavy burden. How many times have you feigned confidence to superiors or reports when you were really unsure? Have you ever felt comfortable conceding that you were confused by the latest business results or caught off guard by a competitor's move? Would you ever admit to feeling inadequate to cope with the complex issues your firm was facing? Anyone who can identify with these situations knows firsthand what it's like to be trapped in the myth of the complete leader—the person at the top without flaws. It's time to put that myth to rest, not only for the sake of frustrated leaders but also for the health of organizations. Even the most talented leaders require the input and leadership of others, constructively solicited and creatively applied. It's time to celebrate the incomplete—that is, the human—leader.

Originally published in February 2007. Reprint R0702E

Using the Balanced Scorecard as a Strategic Management System

by Robert S. Kaplan and David P. Norton

AS COMPANIES AROUND the world transform themselves for competition that is based on information, their ability to exploit intangible assets has become far more decisive than their ability to invest in and manage physical assets. Several years ago, in recognition of this change, we introduced a concept we called the *balanced scorecard*. The balanced scorecard supplemented traditional financial measures with criteria that measured performance from three additional perspectives—those of customers, internal business processes, and learning and growth. (See "Translating vision and strategy: four perspectives.") It therefore enabled companies to track financial results while simultaneously monitoring progress in building the capabilities and acquiring the intangible assets they would need for future growth. The scorecard wasn't a replacement for financial measures; it was their complement.

Recently, we have seen some companies move beyond our early vision for the scorecard to discover its value as the cornerstone of a new strategic management system. Used this way, the scorecard addresses a serious deficiency in traditional management systems: their inability to link a company's long-term strategy with its short-term actions.

Most companies' operational and management control systems are built around financial measures and targets, which bear little relation to the company's progress in achieving long-term strategic objectives. Thus the emphasis most companies place on short-term financial measures leaves a gap between the development of a strategy and its implementation.

Managers using the balanced scorecard do not have to rely on short-term financial measures as the sole indicators of the company's performance. The scorecard lets them introduce four new management processes that, separately and in combination, contribute to linking long-term strategic objectives with short-term actions. (See "Managing strategy: four processes.")

The first new process—*translating the vision*—helps managers build a consensus around the organization's vision and strategy. Despite the best intentions of those at the top, lofty statements about becoming "best in class," "the number one supplier," or an "empowered organization" don't translate easily into operational terms that provide useful guides to action at the local level. For people to act on the words in vision and strategy statements, those statements must be expressed as an integrated set of objectives and measures, agreed upon by all senior executives, that describe the long-term drivers of success.

The second process—*communicating and linking*—lets managers communicate their strategy up and down the organization and link it to departmental and individual objectives. Traditionally, departments are evaluated by their financial performance, and individual incentives are tied to short-term financial goals. The scorecard gives managers a way of ensuring that all levels of the organization understand the long-term strategy and that both departmental and individual objectives are aligned with it.

The third process—*business planning*—enables companies to integrate their business and financial plans. Almost all organizations today are implementing a variety of change programs, each with its

Idea in Brief

Why do budgets often bear little direct relation to a company's long-term strategic objectives? Because they don't take enough into consideration. A balanced scorecard augments traditional financial measures with benchmarks for performance in three key nonfinancial areas:

- a company's relationship with its customers

- its key internal processes

- its learning and growth.

When performance measures for these areas are added to the financial metrics, the result is not only a broader perspective on the company's health and activities, it's also a powerful organizing framework. A sophisticated instrument panel for coordinating and fine-tuning a company's operations and businesses so that all activities are aligned with its strategy.

own champions, gurus, and consultants, and each competing for senior executives' time, energy, and resources. Managers find it difficult to integrate those diverse initiatives to achieve their strategic goals—a situation that leads to frequent disappointments with the programs' results. But when managers use the ambitious goals set for balanced scorecard measures as the basis for allocating resources and setting priorities, they can undertake and coordinate only those initiatives that move them toward their long-term strategic objectives.

The fourth process—*feedback and learning*—gives companies the capacity for what we call strategic learning. Existing feedback and review processes focus on whether the company, its departments, or its individual employees have met their budgeted financial goals. With the balanced scorecard at the center of its management systems, a company can monitor short-term results from the three additional perspectives—customers, internal business processes, and learning and growth—and evaluate strategy in the light of recent performance. The scorecard thus enables companies to modify strategies to reflect real-time learning.

Idea in Practice

The balanced scorecard relies on four processes to bind short-term activities to long-term objectives:

1. Translating the Vision

By relying on measurement, the scorecard forces managers to come to agreement on the metrics they will use to operationalize their lofty visions.

> *Example:* A bank had articulated its strategy as providing "superior service to targeted customers." But the process of choosing operational measures for the four areas of the scorecard made executives realize that they first needed to reconcile divergent views of who the targeted customers were

and what constituted superior service.

2. Communicating and Linking

When a scorecard is disseminated up and down the organizational chart, strategy becomes a tool available to everyone. As the high-level scorecard cascades down to individual business units, overarching strategic objectives and measures are translated into objectives and measures appropriate to each particular group. Tying these targets to individual performance and compensation systems yields "personal scorecards." Thus, individual employees understand how their own productivity supports the overall strategy.

None of the more than 100 organizations that we have studied or with which we have worked implemented their first balanced scorecard with the intention of developing a new strategic management system. But in each one, the senior executives discovered that the scorecard supplied a framework and thus a focus for many critical management processes: departmental and individual goal setting, business planning, capital allocations, strategic initiatives, and feedback and learning. Previously, those processes were uncoordinated and often directed at short-term operational goals. By building the scorecard, the senior executives started a process of change that has gone well beyond the original idea of simply broadening the company's performance measures.

For example, one insurance company—let's call it National Insurance—developed its first balanced scorecard to create a new vision for itself as an underwriting specialist. But once National started to use it, the scorecard allowed the CEO and the senior

3. Business Planning

Most companies have separate procedures (and sometimes units) for strategic planning and budgeting. Little wonder, then, that typical long-term planning is, in the words of one executive, where "the rubber meets the sky." The discipline of creating a balanced scorecard forces companies to integrate the two functions, thereby ensuring that financial budgets do indeed support strategic goals. After agreeing on performance measures for the four scorecard perspectives, companies identify the most influential "drivers" of the desired outcomes and then set milestones for gauging the progress they make with these drivers.

4. Feedback and Learning

By supplying a mechanism for strategic feedback and review, the balanced scorecard helps an organization foster a kind of learning often missing in companies: the ability to reflect on inferences and adjust theories about cause-and-effect relationships.

Feedback about products and services. New learning about key internal processes. Technological discoveries. All this information can be fed into the scorecard, enabling strategic refinements to be made continually. Thus, at any point in the implementation, managers can know whether the strategy is working—and if not, why.

management team not only to introduce a new strategy for the organization but also to overhaul the company's management system. The CEO subsequently told employees in a letter addressed to the whole organization that National would thenceforth use the balanced scorecard and the philosophy that it represented to manage the business.

National built its new strategic management system step-by-step over 30 months, with each step representing an incremental improvement. (See "How one company built a strategic management system . . .") The iterative sequence of actions enabled the company to reconsider each of the four new management processes two or three times before the system stabilized and became an established part of National's overall management system. Thus the CEO was able to transform the company so that everyone could focus on achieving long-term strategic objectives—something that no purely financial framework could do.

Translating vision and strategy: four perspectives

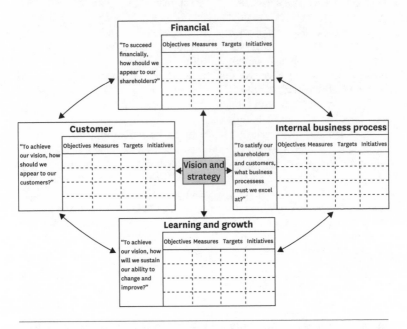

Translating the Vision

The CEO of an engineering construction company, after working with his senior management team for several months to develop a mission statement, got a phone call from a project manager in the field. "I want you to know," the distraught manager said, "that I believe in the mission statement. I want to act in accordance with the mission statement. I'm here with my customer. What am I supposed to do?"

The mission statement, like those of many other organizations, had declared an intention to "use high-quality employees to provide services that surpass customers' needs." But the project manager in the field with his employees and his customer did not know how to translate those words into the appropriate actions. The phone call convinced the CEO that a large gap existed between

Managing strategy: four processes

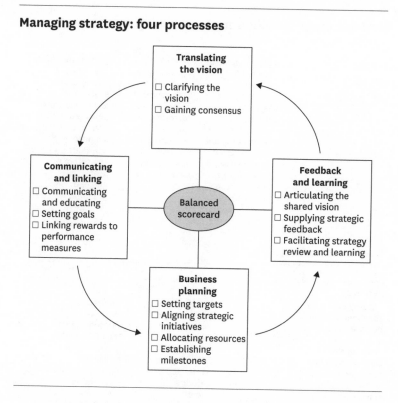

the mission statement and employees' knowledge of how their day-to-day actions could contribute to realizing the company's vision.

Metro Bank (not its real name), the result of a merger of two competitors, encountered a similar gap while building its balanced scorecard. The senior executive group thought it had reached agreement on the new organization's overall strategy: "to provide superior service to targeted customers." Research had revealed five basic market segments among existing and potential customers, each with different needs. While formulating the measures for the customer-perspective portion of their balanced scorecard, however, it became apparent that although the 25 senior executives agreed on the words

How one company built a strategic management system ...

2A *Communicate to middle managers.* The top three layers of management (100 people) are brought together to learn about and discuss the new strategy. The balanced scorecard is the communication vehicle. *(months 4–5)*

2B *Develop business unit scorecards.* Using the corporate scorecard as a template, each business unit translates its strategy into its own scorecard. *(months 6–9)*

5 *Refine the vision.* The review of business unit scorecards identifies several cross-business issues not initially included in the corporate strategy. The corporate scorecard is updated. *(month 12)*

Time frame *(in months)*

0	1	2	3	4	5	6	7	8	9	10	11	12

Actions:

1 *Clarify the vision.* Ten members of a newly formed executive team work together for three months. A balanced scorecard is developed to translate a generic vision into a strategy that is understood and can be communicated. The process helps build consensus and commitment to the strategy.

3A *Eliminate nonstrategic investments.* The corporate scorecard, by clarifying strategic priorities, identifies many active programs that are not contributing to the strategy. *(month 6)*

3B *Launch corporate change programs.* The corporate scorecard identifies the need for cross-business change programs. They are launched while the business units prepare their scorecards. *(month 6)*

4 *Review business unit scorecards.* The CEO and the executive team review the individual business units' scorecards. The review permits the CEO to participate knowledgeably in shaping business unit strategy. *(months 9–11)*

7 *Update long-range plan and budget.* Five-year goals are established for each measure. The investments required to meet those goals are identified and funded. The first year of the five-year plan becomes the annual budget. *(months 15–17)*

9 *Conduct annual strategy review.* At the start of the third year, the initial strategy has been achieved and the corporate strategy requires updating. The executive committee lists ten strategic issues. Each business unit is asked to develop a position on each issue as a prelude to updating its strategy and scorecard. *(months 25–26)*

13	14	15	16	17	18	19	20	21	22	23	24	25	26

6A *Communicate the balanced scorecard to the entire company.* At the end of one year, when the management teams are comfortable with the strategic approach, the scorecard is disseminated to the entire organization. *(month 12–ongoing)*

6B *Establish individual performance objectives.* The top three layers of management link their individual objectives and incentive compensation to their scorecards. *(months 13–14)*

8 *Conduct monthly and quarterly reviews.* After corporate approval of the business unit scorecards, a monthly review process, supplemented by quarterly reviews that focus more heavily on strategic issues, begins. *(month 18–ongoing)*

10 *Link everyone's performance to the balanced scorecard.* All employees are asked to link their individual objectives to the balanced scorecard. The entire organization's incentive compensation is linked to the scorecard. *(months 25–26)*

Note: Steps 7, 8, 9, and 10 are performed on a regular schedule. The balanced scorecard is now a routine part of the management process.

. . . around the balanced scorecard

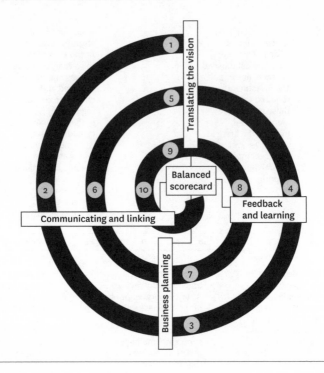

of the strategy, each one had a different definition of *superior service* and a different image of the *targeted customers*.

The exercise of developing operational measures for the four perspectives on the bank's scorecard forced the 25 executives to clarify the meaning of the strategy statement. Ultimately, they agreed to stimulate revenue growth through new products and services and also agreed on the three most desirable customer segments. They developed scorecard measures for the specific products and services that should be delivered to customers in the targeted segments as well as for the relationship the bank should build with customers in each segment. The scorecard also highlighted gaps in employees' skills and in information systems that the bank would have to close in order to deliver the selected value propositions to the targeted customers. Thus, creating a balanced scorecard forced the bank's senior managers to arrive at a consensus and then to translate their vision into terms that had meaning to the people who would realize the vision.

Communicating and Linking

"The top ten people in the business now understand the strategy better than ever before. It's too bad," a senior executive of a major oil company complained, "that we can't put this in a bottle so that everyone could share it." With the balanced scorecard, he can.

One company we have worked with deliberately involved three layers of management in the creation of its balanced scorecard. The senior executive group formulated the financial and customer objectives. It then mobilized the talent and information in the next two levels of managers by having them formulate the internal-business-process and learning-and-growth objectives that would drive the achievement of the financial and customer goals. For example, knowing the importance of satisfying customers' expectations of on-time delivery, the broader group identified several internal business processes—such as order processing, scheduling, and fulfillment—in which the company had to excel. To do so, the company would have to retrain frontline employees and improve the information systems available to them. The group developed performance measures for those critical processes and for staff and systems capabilities.

Broad participation in creating a scorecard takes longer, but it offers several advantages: Information from a larger number of managers is incorporated into the internal objectives; the managers gain a better understanding of the company's long-term strategic goals; and such broad participation builds a stronger commitment to achieving those goals. But getting managers to buy into the scorecard is only a first step in linking individual actions to corporate goals.

The balanced scorecard signals to everyone what the organization is trying to achieve for shareholders and customers alike. But to align employees' individual performances with the overall strategy, scorecard users generally engage in three activities: communicating and educating, setting goals, and linking rewards to performance measures.

Communicating and educating
Implementing a strategy begins with educating those who have to execute it. Whereas some organizations opt to hold their strategy close to the vest, most believe that they should disseminate it from top to bottom. A broad-based communication program shares with all employees the strategy and the critical objectives they have to meet if the strategy is to succeed. Onetime events such as the distribution of brochures or newsletters and the holding of "town meetings" might kick off the program. Some organizations post bulletin boards that illustrate and explain the balanced scorecard measures, then update them with monthly results. Others use groupware and electronic bulletin boards to distribute the scorecard to the desktops of all employees and to encourage dialogue about the measures. The same media allow employees to make suggestions for achieving or exceeding the targets.

The balanced scorecard, as the embodiment of business unit strategy, should also be communicated upward in the organization—to corporate headquarters and to the corporate board of directors. With the scorecard, business units can quantify and communicate their long-term strategies to senior executives using a comprehensive set of linked financial and nonfinancial measures. Such communication informs the executives and the board in specific terms that long-term strategies designed for competitive success are in place. The measures also provide the basis for feedback and accountability. Meeting short-term financial targets should not constitute satisfactory performance when other measures indicate that the long-term strategy is either not working or not being implemented well.

Should the balanced scorecard be communicated beyond the boardroom to external shareholders? We believe that as senior executives gain confidence in the ability of the scorecard measures to monitor strategic performance and predict future financial performance, they will find ways to inform outside investors about those measures without disclosing competitively sensitive information.

Skandia, an insurance and financial services company based in Sweden, issues a supplement to its annual report called "The Business Navigator"—"an instrument to help us navigate into the future and thereby stimulate renewal and development." The supplement describes Skandia's strategy and the strategic measures the company uses to communicate and evaluate the strategy. It also provides a report on the company's performance along those measures during the year. The measures are customized for each operating unit and include, for example, market share, customer satisfaction and retention, employee competence, employee empowerment, and technology deployment.

Communicating the balanced scorecard promotes commitment and accountability to the business's long-term strategy. As one executive at Metro Bank declared, "The balanced scorecard is both motivating and obligating."

Setting goals

Mere awareness of corporate goals, however, is not enough to change many people's behavior. Somehow, the organization's high-level strategic objectives and measures must be translated into objectives and measures for operating units and individuals.

The exploration group of a large oil company developed a technique to enable and encourage individuals to set goals for themselves that were consistent with the organization's. It created a small, fold-up, personal scorecard that people could carry in their shirt pockets or wallets. (See "The personal scorecard.") The scorecard contains three levels of information. The first describes corporate objectives, measures, and targets. The second leaves room for translating corporate targets into targets for each business unit. For the third level, the company asks both individuals and teams to articulate which of their own objectives would be consistent with the business unit and corporate objectives, as well as what initiatives they would take to achieve their objectives. It also asks them to define up to five performance measures for their objectives and to set targets for each measure. The personal scorecard helps to communicate corporate and business unit objectives to the people and teams performing the work, enabling them to translate the objectives into meaningful tasks and targets for themselves. It also lets them keep that information close at hand—in their pockets.

Linking rewards to performance measures

Should compensation systems be linked to balanced scorecard measures? Some companies, believing that tying financial compensation to performance is a powerful lever, have moved quickly to establish such a linkage. For example, an oil company that we'll call Pioneer Petroleum uses its scorecard as the sole basis for computing incentive compensation. The company ties 60% of its executives' bonuses to their achievement of ambitious targets for a weighted average of four financial indicators: return on capital, profitability, cash flow, and operating cost. It bases the remaining 40% on indicators of customer satisfaction, dealer satisfaction, employee satisfaction, and environmental responsibility (such as a percentage change in the level of emissions to water and air). Pioneer's CEO says that linking compensation to the scorecard has helped to align the company with its strategy. "I know of no competitor," he says, "who has this degree of alignment. It is producing results for us."

As attractive and as powerful as such linkage is, it nonetheless carries risks. For instance, does the company have the right measures on the scorecard? Does it have valid and reliable data for the selected measures? Could unintended or unexpected consequences arise from the way the targets for the measures are achieved? Those are questions that companies should ask.

Furthermore, companies traditionally handle multiple objectives in a compensation formula by assigning weights to each objective and calculating incentive compensation by the extent to which each weighted objective was achieved. This practice permits substantial incentive compensation to be paid if the business unit overachieves on a few objectives even if it falls far short on others. A better approach would be to establish minimum threshold levels for a critical subset of the strategic measures. Individuals would earn no

The personal scorecard

Corporate objectives

- ☐ Double our corporate value in seven years.
- ☐ Increase our earnings by an average of 20% per year.
- ☐ Achieve an internal rate of return 2% above the cost of capital.
- ☐ Increase both production and reserves by 20% in the next decade.

Corporate targets					Scorecard measures	Business unit targets					Team/individual objectives and initiatives
1995	1996	1997	1998	1999		1995	1996	1997	1998	1999	
					Financial						1.
100	120	160	180	250	Earnings (in $ millions)						
100	450	200	210	225	Net cash flow						
100	85	80	75	70	Overhead and operating expenses						2.
					Operating						
100	75	73	70	64	Production costs per barrel						
100	97	93	90	82	Development costs per barrel						3.
100	105	108	108	110	Total annual production						
					Team/individual measures				Targets		
					1.						4.
					2.						
					3.						
					4.						5.
					5.						
					Name:						
					Location:						

incentive compensation if performance in a given period fell short of any threshold. This requirement should motivate people to achieve a more balanced performance across short- and long-term objectives.

Some organizations, however, have reduced their emphasis on short-term, formula-based incentive systems as a result of introducing the balanced scorecard. They have discovered that dialogue among executives and managers about the scorecard—both the formulation of the measures and objectives and the explanation of actual versus targeted results—provides a better opportunity to observe managers' performance and abilities. Increased knowledge of their managers' abilities makes it easier for executives to set incentive rewards subjectively and to defend those subjective evaluations—a process that is less susceptible to the game playing and distortions associated with explicit, formula-based rules.

One company we have studied takes an intermediate position. It bases bonuses for business unit managers on two equally weighted criteria: their achievement of a financial objective—economic value added—over a three-year period and a subjective assessment of their performance on measures drawn from the customer, internal-business-process, and learning-and-growth perspectives of the balanced scorecard.

That the balanced scorecard has a role to play in the determination of incentive compensation is not in doubt. Precisely what that role should be will become clearer as more companies experiment with linking rewards to scorecard measures.

Business Planning

"Where the rubber meets the sky": That's how one senior executive describes his company's long-range-planning process. He might have said the same of many other companies because their financially based management systems fail to link change programs and resource allocation to long-term strategic priorities.

The problem is that most organizations have separate procedures and organizational units for strategic planning and for resource allocation and budgeting. To formulate their strategic plans, senior executives go off-site annually and engage for several days in active discussions facilitated by senior planning and development managers or external consultants. The outcome of this exercise is a strategic plan articulating where the company expects (or hopes or prays) to be in three, five, and ten years. Typically, such plans then sit on executives' bookshelves for the next 12 months.

Meanwhile, a separate resource-allocation and budgeting process run by the finance staff sets financial targets for revenues, expenses, profits, and investments for the next fiscal year. The budget it produces consists almost entirely of financial numbers that generally bear little relation to the targets in the strategic plan.

Which document do corporate managers discuss in their monthly and quarterly meetings during the following year? Usually only the budget, because the periodic reviews focus on a comparison of actual and budgeted results for every line item. When is the strategic plan next discussed? Probably during the next annual off-site meeting, when the senior managers draw up a new set of three-, five-, and ten-year plans.

The very exercise of creating a balanced scorecard forces companies to integrate their strategic planning and budgeting processes and therefore helps to ensure that their budgets support their strategies. Scorecard users select measures of progress from all four scorecard perspectives and set targets for each of them. Then they determine which actions will drive them toward their targets, identify the measures they will apply to those drivers from the four perspectives, and establish the short-term milestones that will mark their progress along the strategic paths they have selected. Building a scorecard thus enables a company to link its financial budgets with its strategic goals.

For example, one division of the Style Company (not its real name) committed to achieving a seemingly impossible goal articulated by the CEO: to double revenues in five years. The forecasts built into the organization's existing strategic plan fell $1 billion short of this objective. The division's managers, after considering various scenarios, agreed to specific increases in five different performance drivers: the number of new stores opened, the number of new customers attracted into new and existing stores, the percentage of shoppers in each store converted into actual purchasers, the portion of existing customers retained, and average sales per customer.

By helping to define the key drivers of revenue growth and by committing to targets for each of them, the division's managers eventually grew comfortable with the CEO's ambitious goal.

The process of building a balanced scorecard—clarifying the strategic objectives and then identifying the few critical drivers—also creates a framework for managing an organization's various change programs. These initiatives—reengineering, employee empowerment, time-based management, and total quality management, among others—promise to deliver results but also compete with one another for scarce resources, including the scarcest resource of all: senior managers' time and attention.

Shortly after the merger that created it, Metro Bank, for example, launched more than 70 different initiatives. The initiatives were intended to produce a more competitive and successful institution, but they were inadequately integrated into the overall strategy. After building their balanced scorecard, Metro Bank's managers dropped many of those programs—such as a marketing effort directed at individuals with very high net worth—and consolidated others into initiatives that were better aligned with the company's strategic objectives. For example, the managers replaced a program aimed at enhancing existing low-level selling skills with a major initiative aimed at retraining salespersons to become trusted financial advisers, capable of selling a broad range of newly introduced products to the three selected customer segments. The bank made both changes because the scorecard enabled it to gain a better understanding of the programs required to achieve its strategic objectives.

Once the strategy is defined and the drivers are identified, the scorecard influences managers to concentrate on improving or reengineering those processes most critical to the organization's strategic success. That is how the scorecard most clearly links and aligns action with strategy.

The final step in linking strategy to actions is to establish specific short-term targets, or milestones, for the balanced scorecard measures. Milestones are tangible expressions of managers' beliefs about when and to what degree their current programs will affect those measures.

In establishing milestones, managers are expanding the traditional budgeting process to incorporate strategic as well as financial goals. Detailed financial planning remains important, but financial goals taken by themselves ignore the three other balanced scorecard perspectives. In an integrated planning and budgeting process, executives continue to budget for short-term financial performance, but they also introduce short-term targets for measures in the customer, internal-business-process, and learning-and-growth perspectives. With those milestones established, managers can continually test both the theory underlying the strategy and the strategy's implementation.

At the end of the business-planning process, managers should have set targets for the long-term objectives they would like to achieve in all four scorecard perspectives; they should have identified the strategic initiatives required and allocated the necessary resources to those initiatives; and they should have established milestones for the measures that mark progress toward achieving their strategic goals.

Feedback and Learning

"With the balanced scorecard," a CEO of an engineering company told us, "I can continually test my strategy. It's like performing real-time research." That is exactly the capability that the scorecard should give senior managers: the ability to know at any point in its implementation whether the strategy they have formulated is, in fact, working, and if not, why.

The first three management processes—translating the vision, communicating and linking, and business planning—are vital for implementing strategy, but they are not sufficient in an unpredictable world. Together they form an important single-loop-learning process—single-loop in the sense that the objective remains constant, and any departure from the planned trajectory is seen as a defect to be remedied. This single-loop process does not require or even facilitate reexamination of either the strategy or the techniques used to implement it in light of current conditions.

Most companies today operate in a turbulent environment with complex strategies that, though valid when they were launched, may lose their validity as business conditions change. In this kind of environment, where new threats and opportunities arise constantly, companies must become capable of what Chris Argyris calls *double-loop learning*—learning that produces a change in people's assumptions and theories about cause-and-effect relationships. (See "Teaching Smart People How to Learn," HBR May–June 1991.)

Budget reviews and other financially based management tools cannot engage senior executives in double-loop learning—first, because these tools address performance from only one perspective, and second, because they don't involve strategic learning. Strategic learning consists of gathering feedback, testing the hypotheses on which strategy was based, and making the necessary adjustments.

The balanced scorecard supplies three elements that are essential to strategic learning. First, it articulates the company's shared vision, defining in clear and operational terms the results that the company, as a team, is trying to achieve. The scorecard communicates a holistic model that links individual efforts and accomplishments to business unit objectives.

Second, the scorecard supplies the essential strategic feedback system. A business strategy can be viewed as a set of hypotheses about cause-and-effect relationships. A strategic feedback system should be able to test, validate, and modify the hypotheses embedded in a business unit's strategy. By establishing short-term goals, or milestones, within the business-planning process, executives are forecasting the relationship between changes in performance drivers and the associated changes in one or more specified goals. For example, executives at Metro Bank estimated the amount of time it would take for improvements in training and in the availability of information systems before employees could sell multiple financial products effectively to existing and new customers. They also estimated how great the effect of that selling capability would be.

Another organization attempted to validate its hypothesized cause-and-effect relationships in the balanced scorecard by measuring the strength of the linkages among measures in the different perspectives. (See the exhibit "How one company linked measures from the four perspectives.") The company found significant correlations between employees' morale, a measure in the learning-and-growth perspective, and customer satisfaction, an important customer perspective measure. Customer satisfaction, in turn, was correlated with faster payment of invoices—a relationship that led to a substantial reduction in accounts receivable and hence a higher return on capital employed. The company also found correlations between employees' morale and the number of suggestions made by employees (two learning-and-growth measures) as well as between an increased number of suggestions and lower rework (an internal-business-process measure). Evidence of such strong correlations help to confirm the organization's business strategy. If, however, the expected correlations are not found over time, it should be an indication to executives that the theory underlying the unit's strategy may not be working as they had anticipated.

Especially in large organizations, accumulating sufficient data to document significant correlations and causation among balanced scorecard measures can take a long time—months or years. Over the short term, managers' assessment of strategic impact may have to rest on subjective and qualitative judgments. Eventually, however, as more evidence accumulates, organizations may be able to provide more objectively grounded estimates of cause-and-effect relationships. But just getting managers to think systematically about the assumptions underlying their strategy is an improvement over the current practice of making decisions based on short-term operational results.

Third, the scorecard facilitates the strategy review that is essential to strategic learning. Traditionally, companies use the monthly or quarterly meetings between corporate and division executives to analyze the most recent period's financial results. Discussions focus on past performance and on explanations of why financial objectives were not achieved. The balanced scorecard, with its specification of the causal relationships between performance drivers and objectives, allows corporate and business unit executives to use their periodic review sessions to evaluate the validity of the unit's strategy and the quality of its execution. If the unit's employees and

How one company linked measures from the four perspectives

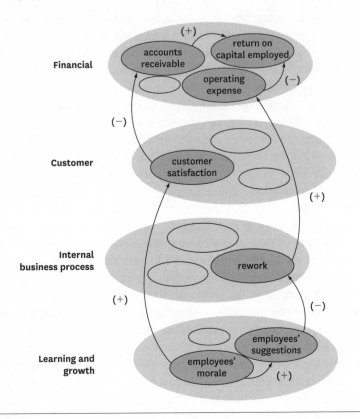

managers have delivered on the performance drivers (retraining of employees, availability of information systems, and new financial products and services, for instance), then their failure to achieve the expected outcomes (higher sales to targeted customers, for example) signals that the theory underlying the strategy may not be valid. The disappointing sales figures are an early warning.

Managers should take such disconfirming evidence seriously and reconsider their shared conclusions about market conditions, customer value propositions, competitors' behavior, and internal capabilities. The result of such a review may be a decision to reaffirm their belief in the current strategy but to adjust the quantitative relationship among the strategic measures on the balanced scorecard. But they also might conclude that the unit needs a different strategy (an example of double-loop learning) in light of new knowledge about market conditions and internal capabilities. In any case, the scorecard will have stimulated key executives to learn about the viability of their strategy. This capacity for enabling organizational learning at the executive level—strategic learning—is what distinguishes the balanced scorecard, making it invaluable for those who wish to create a strategic management system.

Toward a New Strategic Management System

Many companies adopted early balanced scorecard concepts to improve their performance measurement systems. They achieved tangible but narrow results. Adopting those concepts provided clarification, consensus, and focus on the desired improvements in performance. More recently, we have seen companies expand their use of the balanced scorecard, employing it as the foundation of an integrated and iterative strategic management system. Companies are using the scorecard to

- clarify and update strategy;
- communicate strategy throughout the company;
- align unit and individual goals with the strategy;
- link strategic objectives to long-term targets and annual budgets;
- identify and align strategic initiatives; and
- conduct periodic performance reviews to learn about and improve strategy.

The balanced scorecard enables a company to align its management processes and focuses the entire organization on implementing long-term strategy. At National Insurance, the scorecard provided the CEO and his managers with a central framework around which they could redesign each piece of the company's management system. And because of the cause-and-effect linkages inherent in the scorecard framework, changes in one component of the system reinforced earlier changes made elsewhere. Therefore, every change made over the 30-month period added to the momentum that kept the organization moving forward in the agreed-upon direction.

Without a balanced scorecard, most organizations are unable to achieve a similar consistency of vision and action as they attempt to change direction and introduce new strategies and processes. The balanced scorecard provides a framework for managing the implementation of strategy while also allowing the strategy itself to evolve in response to changes in the company's competitive, market, and technological environments.

Originally published in January 1996. Reprint R0707M.

Health Care's Service Fanatics

How the Cleveland Clinic Leaped to the Top of Patient-Satisfaction Surveys.

by James I. Merlino and Ananth Raman

THE CLEVELAND CLINIC has long had a reputation for medical excellence and for holding down costs. But in 2009 Delos "Toby" Cosgrove, the CEO, examined its performance relative to that of other hospitals and admitted to himself that inpatients did not think much of their experience at its flagship medical center or its eight community hospitals—and decided something had to be done. Over the next three years the Clinic transformed itself. Its overall ranking in the Centers for Medicare & Medicaid Services (CMS) survey of patient satisfaction jumped from about average to among the top 8% of the roughly 4,600 hospitals included. Hospital executives from all over the world now flock to Cleveland to study the Clinic's practices and to learn how it changed.

The Clinic's journey also holds lessons for organizations outside health care—ones that until now have not had to compete by creating a superior experience for customers. Such enterprises often have workforces that were not hired with customer satisfaction in mind. Can they improve the customer experience without jeopardizing their traditional strengths? The Clinic's success suggests that they can.

The Cleveland Clinic's transformation involved actions any organization can take. Cosgrove made improving the patient experience a strategic priority, ultimately appointing James Merlino, a prominent colorectal surgeon (and a coauthor of this piece), to lead the effort. By spelling out the problems in a systematic, sustained fashion, Merlino got everyone in the enterprise—including physicians who thought that only medical outcomes mattered—to recognize that patient dissatisfaction was a significant issue and that all employees, even administrators and janitors, were "caregivers" who should play a role in fixing it. By conducting surveys and studies and soliciting patients' input, the Clinic developed a deep understanding of patients' needs. It gave Merlino a dedicated staff and an ample budget with which to change mind-sets, develop and implement processes, create metrics, and monitor performance so that the organization could continually improve. And it communicated intensively with prospective patients to set realistic expectations for what their time in the hospital would be like.

These steps were not rocket science, but they changed the organization very quickly. What's more, fears expressed by some physicians that the initiative might conflict with efforts to maintain high quality and safety standards and to further reduce costs turned out to be unfounded. During the transformation the Clinic rose dramatically in the University HealthSystem Consortium's rankings of 97 academic medical centers on quality and safety. Its efficiency in delivering care improved as well.

Founded in 1921 with a single site, the Cleveland Clinic has long been one of the most prestigious medical centers in the United States. It has pioneered many procedures (including cardiac catheterization, open-heart bypass, face transplant, and deep-brain stimulation for psychiatric disorders) and made a number of breakthrough discoveries (identifying genes linked to juvenile macular degeneration and to coronary artery disease, for example). It expanded aggressively in the late 1990s and is now one of the largest nonprofit health care providers in the United States. In addition to its 1,200-bed main hospital and its community hospitals, it has 18 family health centers throughout northeastern Ohio; a tertiary-care hospital in Weston, Florida; a brain treatment center in Las Vegas; and operations in Canada, Abu Dhabi, and Saudi Arabia. In 2012 its

Idea in Brief

Organizations that have not had to compete by offering great customer service but suddenly find that they must do so often face a challenge: They have a culture, employees, and processes ill-suited to the task.

But the Cleveland Clinic's success in transforming itself shows that it can be done. In just a few years the Clinic went from having mediocre patient-satisfaction scores to rising to the upper echelons of U.S. hospitals.

Its CEO made improving patients' experiences a strategic priority. He appointed a prominent physician—an insider who commanded the respect of other physicians (a key interest group)—to lead the effort and gave him ample resources: a staff that now numbers 112 people.

The initiative, which is still under way, is having an additional benefit: helping the Clinic improve quality, safety, and efficiency.

43,000 employees treated 1.3 million people, including more than 50,000 inpatients at the main campus.

For most of the Clinic's history, providing patients with an excellent overall experience—in areas such as making appointments, offering a pleasant physical environment, addressing their fears and concerns during their stays, and providing clear discharge instructions—was not a priority. Like most hospitals, especially prestigious ones, the Clinic focused almost solely on medical outcomes. It took great pride that *U.S. News & World Report* repeatedly ranked it among the top five U.S. hospitals for overall quality of care and listed its heart program as number one.

In 2007 the Clinic adopted a new care model in an effort to improve collaboration and thereby increase quality and efficiency and reduce costs. It abandoned the traditional hospital structure, in which a department of medicine supervises specialties such as cardiology, pulmonology, and gastroenterology while a department of surgery oversees general surgery along with cardiac, transplant, and other specialty procedures. Instead it created institutes in which multidisciplinary teams treat all the conditions affecting a particular organ system. Its heart and vascular institute, for example, includes everything having to do with the heart and circulatory systems (cardiac surgery, cardiology, vascular surgery, and vascular medicine), and cardiologists and surgeons see patients together. The new model had positive effects not only on quality and costs but also on the patient experience.

Certain developments, though, soon led the Clinic's leadership to realize that these changes and accomplishments would not suffice. In 2008, to help consumers make more-informed choices and to encourage hospitals to improve care, the CMS began making the scores in its satisfaction survey and comparative data on the quality of care publicly available online. It announced that starting in 2013, roughly $1 billion in Medicare payments to hospitals would be contingent on performance in these areas, and the amount at risk would double by 2017.

CMS satisfaction scores are based on randomly selected patients' postdischarge responses to questions about how well doctors and nurses communicated with them, whether caregivers treated them with courtesy and respect, the staff's responsiveness to the call button, how well their pain was controlled, and the cleanliness of the room and bathroom, among other things. Patients are also asked to give the hospital an overall rating and to say whether they would recommend it to friends and family.

The Clinic's overall score was just average that year, and its performance in some areas was downright dismal: It ranked in the bottom 4% for staff responsiveness and room cleanliness, 5% for whether the area near a patient's room was quiet at night, 14% for doctors' communication skills, and 16% for nurses' communication skills. "Patients were coming to us for the clinical excellence, but they did not like us very much," Cosgrove says. And from stories he'd heard from patients and their families and consumer research he had read, he realized that he couldn't count on medical excellence to continue attracting patients—for many people choosing a hospital, the anticipated patient experience trumped medical excellence. He decided to make improving the patient experience an enterprisewide priority.

Leading the Change

Cosgrove understood that to achieve that goal, the Clinic would need to significantly change how it operated. Getting employees to modify their mind-sets and behaviors wouldn't be easy. In recent years cost pressures had forced hospitals to cut support staff even as medical complexity and regulatory demands increased. Launching an initiative that would add to the burden would be challenging. Obtaining buy-in from physicians would be especially difficult. The Clinic differs from many hospitals in that its physicians are employees, but they wield more power than employees often do. Many are superstars in their specialties; they are a major reason—maybe *the* reason—patients choose the Clinic. Cosgrove couldn't expect to issue an edict and have them salute and obey.

For all those reasons, he decided to create a new position, chief experience officer. He initially appointed an outsider who was not a practicing physician. She left after 24 months. He then decided to call on a senior physician from inside the organization—someone who would fully understand the challenges of delivering a great patient experience while also focusing on medical outcomes and who would have immediate credibility. He chose Merlino.

Merlino had recently moved his practice from the MetroHealth Medical Center, a large county hospital in Cleveland, to the Clinic, where he'd held a fellowship earlier in his career. He was already working on making the digestive disease institute a "patient-centered" organization. Before building his surgical practice, he had worked in government administration and in political public-opinion research and had served on a community hospital's board.

During his interview with Cosgrove, Merlino told a story about his father, who had been a patient at the Clinic several years earlier. That experience had been terrible: Among other things, his father felt that the nurses had been unresponsive, and his physician had not always seen him daily. He had died in the hospital thinking it was the worst place in the world. "Nobody else should die here believing that," Merlino said. Both men admitted they didn't know what accomplishing that goal would take. "We will need to figure it out together," Merlino told the CEO. Twenty minutes after the interview, Cosgrove's chief of staff called Merlino to offer him the job, asking him to devote 50% of his time to the initiative (he now devotes 80%).

To help carry out the mandate, Cosgrove gave Merlino the Office of Patient Experience, which currently has a $9.2 million annual budget and 112 people, including project managers, data experts, and service excellence trainers. Its responsibilities include conducting and analyzing patient surveys, interpreting patients' complaints, administering "voice of the patient" advisory councils, training employees, and working with units to identify and fix problems.

Publicly Acknowledging the Problem

Getting employees to take the new mandate seriously was a considerable challenge. Doctors and nurses typically focus on performing procedures and treatments and often fail to explain them fully and in terms patients can understand. The Clinic's caregivers were no different.

Ignorance and cost pressures presented two other obstacles. Employees at most hospitals are unaware of CMS scores or don't believe they matter all that much, and they don't understand how to improve the patient experience. Some executives believe incorrectly that amenities like better food and bigger TVs are the key, and others are reluctant to invest scarce funds in a major change program. In these areas, too, the Clinic was no exception.

One of the OPE's first projects under Merlino was to broadly publicize the detailed results of the CMS survey—both for the Clinic as a whole and for individual units. This was Cosgrove's idea. Before becoming CEO, Cosgrove had led the department of cardiothoracic surgery, and he had been tasked with improving the department's surgical outcomes. One method he'd found effective was releasing outcomes data on every surgeon and program so that all could see how their performance compared with that of others. He hoped that publicizing the CMS data would have a similar effect. In one sense, it did: Employees were shocked by the scores and understood that the problem was important. But they were confused about what they could do personally to raise them.

Understanding Patients' Needs

Merlino recognized that to drive meaningful change, he had to create a strategy and a plan for executing it. To measure progress, he decided to rely on the metrics used in the CMS satisfaction surveys—the Hospital Consumer Assessment of Healthcare Providers and Systems. This was an easy choice: The CMS data had credibility, they were available online to consumers, and hospitals' Medicare reimbursements would soon be affected by them. But the industry's understanding of *why* patients graded hospitals as they did—of what patients' underlying needs were—was limited.

The Clinic had tried to make itself more appealing to patients by doing things like having greeters at the door, redesigning its gowns, and improving food services. But these amenities were superficial efforts—and shots in the dark. It was unclear which, if any, affected the CMS scores.

Merlino saw that if the patient experience was going to be a strategic priority, employees had to understand exactly what it meant and what each person's responsibility for delivering it entailed. He crafted a broad, holistic definition: The patient experience was everyone and everything people encountered from the time they decided to go to the Clinic until they were discharged. The effort to improve it became known as "managing the 360."

Although institutions talk a lot about the importance of empathy in delivering good care, they actually have little knowledge of what patients experience as they navigate health care, except for their interactions with doctors and nurses. So Merlino commissioned two studies. The first involved a randomly selected group of former patients who had taken the CMS survey by phone. Researchers followed up with them, asking why they'd answered each question the way they had. The second was an anthropological examination of a nursing unit that had received some of the Clinic's worst scores in the CMS survey. Researchers observed interactions between patients and employees and questioned both parties about things that happened.

The studies produced a number of findings. Although several problem areas were not especially surprising, it was clear that employees did not always keep them in mind. Patients did not want to be in the hospital. They were afraid, sometimes terrified, often confused, and always anxious. They wanted reassurance that the people taking care of them really understood what it was like to be a patient. Their families felt the same way.

Patients also wanted better communication: They wanted information about what was going on in their environment and about the plan of care; they wanted to be kept up-to-date even on minute activities. And they wanted better coordination of their care. When nurses and doctors did not communicate with one another, patients were left feeling that no one was taking responsibility for them.

The studies also revealed that patients often used proxies in their ratings: If the room was dirty, for example, they might take it as a sign that the hospital delivered poor care. Another striking finding was the importance of doctors' and nurses' demeanor. Patients tended to be more satisfied when their caregivers were happy. It wasn't that they craved interactions with happy employees; rather, they believed that if their caregivers were unhappy, it meant either that the patient was doing something to make them feel that way or that something was going on that they did not want to reveal.

Making Everyone a Caregiver

At most hospitals the primary relationship is considered to be between the doctor and the patient; the rest of the staff members see themselves in supporting roles. But in the eyes of patients, all their interactions are important.

To understand how many people a patient typically encounters, Merlino asked one patient—a woman undergoing an uncomplicated colorectal surgery—to keep a journal of everyone who cared for her during her five-day stay. It turned out that there were eight doctors, 60 nurses, and so many others (phlebotomists, environmental service workers, transporters, food workers, and house staff) that the patient lost track. Few of her 120 hours at the Clinic were spent with physicians. Moreover, her journal did not even take into account employees in nonclinical areas, such as billing, marketing, parking, and food operations—people who did not interact directly with her but might have had a big impact on her stay. Merlino realized that *all* employees are caregivers, and that the doctor-centric relationship should be replaced by a caregiver-centric one.

To get everyone in the organization to start thinking and acting accordingly, Merlino proposed having all 43,000 employees participate in a half-day exercise. Randomly assembled groups of eight to 10 people would meet around a table with a trained facilitator—a janitor might be seated between a neurosurgeon and a nurse. All would participate as caregivers, sharing stories about what they did—and what they could do better—to put the patient first and to help the Clinic deliver world-class care. They would also be trained in basic behaviors practiced by workers at exemplary service organizations: smiling; telling patients and other staff members their names, roles, and what to expect during the activity in question; actively listening to and assisting patients; building rapport by learning something personal about them; and thanking them. The cost of the half-day program, including the employees' salaries, would be $11 million.

Cosgrove embraced the idea, but some members of the executive team were skeptical. Physicians on the team believed that doctors would never go along with the plan and should not have to take time from their busy schedules. The head of nursing at the time worried about the impact on productivity of taking nurses away from the floor and questioned whether it could be justified without a quantifiable ROI. Cosgrove listened to the discussion in silence and then spoke. Making any exceptions, he said, would undermine one of the program's main aims: to eliminate the divide between doctors and the rest of the staff and create a unified culture in which everyone worked together to do what was best for the patients. And yes, the ROI was unclear. "But what will be the cost [for patients and the organization] of *not* proceeding?" he asked. The executive team acquiesced.

The program was launched in late 2010. It took a full year for everyone to go through it. A handful of physicians asked to be excused but were refused. As hoped, the program had a profound impact. Nonphysician employees were amazed by the experience of sitting with doctors and discussing how they, too, were caregivers. Participants shared frustrations about not always being able to provide a nurturing environment. Even doctors who had been skeptical about the exercise felt it was worthwhile.

Embedding Changes

To continue to drive change and to permanently alter how people performed their jobs, the Clinic instituted a number of other measures:

Identifying problems

Merlino put in place systems to track and analyze patients' attitudes and complaints and to determine and address the root causes of problems. Like many hospitals, the Clinic had used a similar approach to improve safety. Applying the methodology to issues like dirty rooms, noisy environments, and patient-caregiver communication was not a big leap. In addition, the Clinic's business intelligence department set up electronic dashboards that displayed real-time data available for all managers to view.

Establishing processes and norms

Merlino created a "best practices" department within the OPE to identify, implement, promote, and monitor approaches used by top performers in the CMS survey. In many cases it tested practices in pilot projects before rolling them out broadly.

Some efforts were relatively simple. For example, one program reinforced the basic behaviors taught in the half-day exercise. As part of the program, managers monitored their employees and coached those who were falling short.

A related initiative targeted prospective patients—people deciding where to go for care. A common complaint of potential patients who'd opted to go elsewhere was that the Clinic was too big and was difficult to access; people needed a special connection—"to know someone"—to get an appointment. So Cosgrove mandated that all patients have the option of getting an appointment the same day they called, making the Clinic the first major U.S. provider to offer this service. It created a single phone number for booking appointments, and centralized scheduling across the enterprise. When patients called the dedicated number, operators were trained to say, "Thank you for calling the Cleveland Clinic. Would you like to be seen today?" A television and radio advertising campaign, "Today," promoted the new service and sent a clear message that the Clinic would help patients with anything they needed, not just complicated conditions. The campaign was an overnight success: During the first year, visits by new patients increased by 20%. Same-day appointments now account for more than one million patient visits a year.

Another common complaint was that despite the creation of the multidisciplinary institutes, caregivers did not communicate or coordinate well with one another. Merlino decided to begin addressing this problem by testing a process to determine the root causes of communication breakdowns in each unit; remedies would then be devised on a case-by-case basis. He commissioned a study of the weekly huddles of critical floor leaders, selecting for the pilot a floor with one of the hospital's worst scores in the CMS survey. A team consisting of the floor's nurse manager; its assistant nurse manager; a physician from the specialty that had the most patients on the floor; the environmental services supervisor (who oversaw housekeeping); the case manager responsible for discharge, insurance, and at-home needs; a social worker; and a representative from the Office of Patient Experience began meeting each week to discuss patient complaints and concerns.

It quickly identified several problems. First, the social worker and the case manager—employees critical to ensuring a smooth discharge process—did not like each other and never talked. The floor, which conducted a large volume of gastroenterology and radiology procedures, constantly ran behind schedule. Patients ordered to have no food or drink before a procedure might go hungry all day if the procedure was delayed; even worse, procedures were sometimes postponed until the next day without the patient's being informed—leaving him or her not just hungry but confused. Finally, doctors did not always communicate with nurses after rounds, so nurses were often unaware of the plans for their patients' care that day.

These problems were not difficult to fix. Most of them were addressed by instituting simple processes to surface issues, get people to work better together, and keep patients informed about what was going on. For example, the weekly huddles forced caregivers to communicate regularly with their colleagues, including ones they did not particularly like. The floor's scores in the CMS survey went from among the lowest in the hospital to the highest in less than a month.

Another area that was hurting the Clinic in the CMS survey was nursing rounds. Rounding on patients hourly is an established best practice that improves safety, quality, and patient satisfaction. But as of 2010 the Clinic did not require hourly rounds; some units conducted them, some didn't. The units that did had higher patient-experience scores, and when the Clinic's leaders learned of the correlation, they decided to launch a pilot project in the heart and vascular institute under the direction of K. Kelly Hancock, who was then its nursing director and is now the Clinic's executive chief nursing officer.

For a period of 90 days, the nurses or nursing assistants on designated floors were required to see patients every hour and to ask them five questions: Do you need anything? Do you have any pain? Do you need to be repositioned? Do you need your personal belongings moved closer to you? Do you need to go to the bathroom? They had to fill out sheets verifying that they had done this. Nurse managers held spot audits, and patients being discharged were asked if the rounds had been performed. Some 4,000 patients in all were involved, and the results were striking. The units that always completed the rounds ranked in the top 10% in the nursing-related parts of the CMS survey; the units that conducted rounds inconsistently scored much lower. The units that never conducted hourly rounds ranked in the bottom 1% of all hospitals. So Cosgrove mandated hourly rounds across the institution.

Engaging and motivating employees

The leaders of the Clinic knew that to improve the patient experience while continuing to drive safety and quality, it would need engaged, satisfied caregivers who understood and identified with its mission: providing exemplary care by excelling in specialized care; developing, applying, evaluating, and sharing new technology; attracting the best staff; excelling in service; and providing efficient access to affordable care. A 2008 Gallup survey of employee engagement at health care organizations highlighted the magnitude of the problem in this regard: The Clinic placed only in the 38th percentile.

One step taken to address this problem was the launching of a "caregiver celebration" program. This allowed both managers and frontline workers to recognize colleagues who had done something exceptional for patients or for the organization. Recognition made employees eligible for monetary awards of varying amounts, culminating in the $25,000 CEO Award of Excellence, presented to the top caregiver and team members at an annual ceremony.

More broadly, Merlino, Cosgrove, and other members of the executive team recognized that they needed to make a substantial investment in developing and managing the workforce. They saw that the organization's 2,300 managers needed to be educated in how to increase the engagement of members of their teams. All managers are now required to attend a daylong session every three or four months, during which they are trained in such things as emotional intelligence, communicating and implementing change, and enhancing engagement. They must submit annual plans for how they will improve the engagement and satisfaction of the people they manage (actions might include discussing job expectations more frequently, improving communication about activities in the department or the Clinic, and ensuring that employees have the resources needed to perform their jobs). Such steps helped the Clinic move up to the 57th percentile in the Gallup survey. Although this is progress, Clinic leaders recognize that it is not nearly enough.

Results of Cleveland Clinic's
Patient-Satisfaction Surveys

How the Cleveland Clinic stacks up: The Clinic's percentile ranking among hospitals surveyed for the proportion of patients who gave their institution the highest possible score. (*Source:* Centers for Medicare & Medicaid Services.)

Overall satisfaction

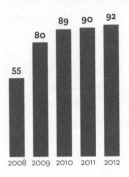

Room cleanliness

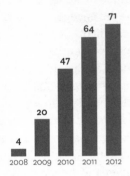

Nurses' communication

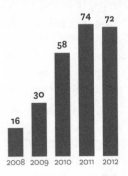

Doctors' communication

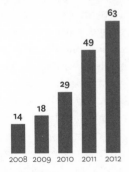

Communication about medication

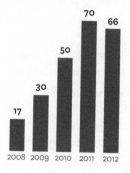

Pain management

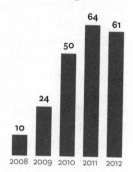

Quiet at night

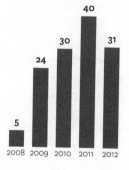

Discharge information

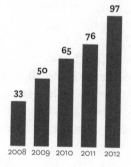

Staff responsiveness

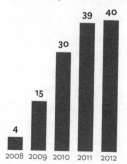

Setting Patients' Expectations

The patient is not always right: Sometimes patients have desires whose fulfillment would not be in their best interests. Here's a case in point: Patients understandably prefer not to be disturbed at night. But sometimes they must be awakened in order to be given medication, to have a procedure performed, or to have their vital signs checked. Because some patients at the Clinic did not understand the reasons for such disturbances, they were critical when asked in the CMS survey whether their rooms had been quiet at night.

Similarly, the OPE discovered that patients were upset if they used the call system to ask for a nurse's help and did not receive an immediate response—even if their need wasn't pressing. When it probed deeper, it learned that even when patients recognized that their need wasn't urgent, the lack of an immediate response often made them anxious—many feared that if there *were* an emergency, nobody would come. They didn't know that the person answering calls prioritizes them according to the urgency of the request.

The Clinic found it could alleviate such problems by letting patients know *before* they got to the hospital what to expect while they were there. It created printed materials and an interactive online video for incoming patients, describing the hospital environment and procedures and explaining the rationale for them. It also educated them about pain management and how to communicate with providers.

In addition, Merlino realized that the Clinic could enlist patients' help in improving the hospital experience. For instance, it began asking patients in semiprivate rooms to limit nighttime noise. It started to rely more heavily on patients to identify problems and improve processes. It now asks patients to report rooms that have not been cleaned properly and to routinely ask caregivers if they have washed their hands.

Such measures may seem minor, but the effects are important, in terms of cost as well as patient satisfaction. In 2012 salaries, wages, and benefits totaled 56% of the Clinic's operating revenue (supplies accounted for just 10%, pharmaceuticals for 7%). To hold down costs, hospitals will clearly have to increase employee productivity. One approach that has worked well in retailing and service industries is to encourage customers to perform tasks that employees have traditionally done—for example, booking airline tickets, checking out of stores, and answering other customers' questions. If such a process is designed empathically, it can enhance patients' experiences even as it reduces costs.

Hospital leaders may believe that they cannot justify the kinds of programs described here. CMS's linking of Medicare reimbursement to patient satisfaction should help convince them otherwise. They should also remember this: Changing culture and processes to improve the patient experience can lead to substantial improvements in safety and quality. To put it bluntly, a patient-centered approach to care, which includes giving patients an outstanding experience, is not an option; it's a necessity.

Despite the Clinic's progress, its leaders know full well that they cannot proclaim victory. Some obvious shortcomings, such as the still-modest degree of employee engagement, remain. And at a fundamental level, operating a truly patient-centered organization isn't a program; it's a way of life. Doing the best by patients means continually analyzing what can be done better and then figuring out how. There will always be something.

Originally published in May 2013. Reprint R1305J

Engaging Doctors in the Health Care Revolution

by Thomas H. Lee and Toby Cosgrove

DESPITE WONDROUS ADVANCES in medicine and technology, health care regularly fails at the fundamental job of any business: to reliably deliver what its customers need. In the face of ever-increasing complexity, the hard work and best intentions of individual physicians can no longer guarantee efficient, high-quality care. Fixing health care will require a radical transformation, moving from a system organized around individual physicians to a team-based approach focused on patients. Doctors, of course, must be central players in the transformation: Any ambitious strategy that they do not embrace is doomed.

And yet, many physicians are deeply anxious about the changes under way and are mourning real or anticipated losses of autonomy, respect, and income. They are being told that they must accept new organizational structures, ways of working, payment models, and performance goals. They struggle to care for the endless stream of patients who want to be seen, but they constantly hear that much of what they do is waste. They're moving at various rates through the stages of grief: A few are still in denial, but many are in the second stage—anger. Bursts of rage over relatively small issues are common.

Given doctors' angst, how can leaders best engage them in redesigning care? In our roles in senior management of two large U.S. health care systems, and as observers and partners of many others, we have seen firsthand that winning physicians' support takes more than simple incentives. Leaders at all levels must draw on reserves of optimism, courage, and resilience. They must develop an understanding of behavioral economics and social capital and be ready to part company with clinicians who refuse to work with their colleagues to improve outcomes and efficiency.

To help health care leaders engage physicians in the pursuit of their organizations' greater goals, we suggest a framework based on the writings of the economist and sociologist Max Weber, who described four motivations that drive social action (that is, action in response to others' behavior). Adapted for health care professionals, these are: shared purpose, self-interest, respect, and tradition.

TABLE 11-1

Motivational tools that improve engagement

This adaptation of Max Weber's typology of social action describes four motivations that leaders can tap to engage physicians in redesigning health care.

Motivation	How to apply it	Example
To engage in a noble shared purpose	Appeal to the satisfaction of pursuing a common organizational goal.	The Cleveland Clinic reinforced its commitment to compassionate care by launching a same-day appointment policy.
To satisfy self-interest	Provide financial or other rewards for achieving targets.	At Geisinger Health System, 20% of endocrinologists' compensation is tied to goals such as improving control of patients' diabetes.
To earn respect	Leverage peer pressure to encourage desired performance.	Patients' ratings of University of Utah physicians are shared both internally and on public websites to drive improvements in patient experience.
To embrace tradition	Create standards to align behaviors, and make adherence a requirement for community membership.	At the Mayo Clinic, a strict dress code and communication rules signal the "Mayo way of doing things."

See also Nikola Biller-Andorno and Thomas H. Lee, "Ethical Physician Incentives—From Carrots and Sticks to Shared Purpose," *New England Journal of Medicine*, March 2013.

Idea in Brief

The Challenge. Doctors must be central players in the sweeping changes transforming health care. Indeed, any change strategy they do not embrace is doomed. But many fear a loss of autonomy and income and are resistant to change.

The Analysis. Engaging doctors in change requires first clarifying the organizational goal. Leaders must shift the emphasis from the short-term maximization of revenue to the long-term strategy of increasing value, putting what's best for patients first.

The Solution. Leaders can bring doctors along by applying four motivational strategies: engaging them in a noble shared purpose, appealing to their self-interest, leveraging peer pressure to encourage desired performance, and emphasizing organizational traditions to align behaviors.

Leaders can use these levers to earn doctors' buy-in and bring about the change the system so urgently needs.

Getting Started

The first step in any strategic transformation is to clarify the goal. What, exactly, do leaders want physicians to engage with? Traditionally, hospitals have defined physician engagement as the extent to which doctors saw their future as intertwined with that of the larger organization. Hospitals wanted physicians to be loyal— that is, to refer most or all of their patients to them, thereby increasing revenue. Even today, many hospital administrators believe that their true "customers" are the physicians who bring them patients— not the patients themselves. Working with physicians to reduce costs or improve quality is regarded as important, but secondary to increasing volume.

Here we describe a new concept of physician engagement. Such engagement requires more than mere cooperation—an agreement not to sabotage—and strives instead for full collaboration in relentless improvement. To be sure, we still need physicians to work hard as individuals and keep care within the family of the local hospital and physician community. But physician engagement can no longer be about short-term maximization of fee-for-service revenue;

it must further the long-term strategy of improving outcomes and lowering costs—increasing value for patients. (See Michael E. Porter and Thomas H. Lee, "The Strategy That Will Fix Health Care," HBR October 2013.)

Many organizations hope that they can win over physicians by combining good intentions with a few broad interventions, such as putting doctors in leadership roles and creating financial incentives for desired behavior. But as we have seen too often, such uncoordinated, piecemeal efforts are insufficient. Leaders need to tap into all four motivational levers in concert (see "Motivational tools that improve engagement"). They must begin by focusing on shared purpose, without which the pursuit of the other three can seem perverse and may prove ineffective.

Engaging in Shared Purpose

Most discussions about health care these days dwell on its problems—spiraling costs, lack of access, uneven quality—and give short shrift to the possibility of a better future. To help physicians move beyond grief and anger about what they might be losing as the health care system remodels, leaders must shift the conversation to something different—something positive, noble, and important. They must articulate a vision of what lies on the other side of the turmoil ahead: health care that will be better—maybe even great—for patients. Improved patient care has to form the core of any change agenda that clinicians will embrace.

At the same time, health care leaders must frankly acknowledge the need for sacrifice. The journey will be arduous and might reduce autonomy and income for some physicians. But leaders must take the position that achieving the goal of high-value care for every patient is more important than preserving the status quo for any individual physician. The alternative—that the organization will prioritize doctors' interests over patients' and shield doctors from the changes sweeping through health care—is impossible to defend.

Creating such a shared purpose starts with the same steps used to build consensus in any organization: listening, demonstrating respect for diverse views, and creating processes through which stakeholders can help shape the vision's implementation. But health care leaders face additional challenges: About half the physicians in the United States are not employees of the organizations where they provide care, so they don't respond to the perks and threats that managers commonly use to influence employee behavior. What's more, even those who are employees tend not to see themselves that way and view their duty to patients as preempting other obligations.

Far from being an obstacle, however, that perspective can be a path to meaningful change. Health care leaders can engage physicians by putting the focus on patients and their suffering, trumping all other concerns. During Hurricane Sandy and the Boston Marathon bombings, no physician worried about compensation or hours worked. All were solely focused on helping patients. In less dramatic contexts, when faced with individual patients whose lives are in crisis, a physician's instinct is similarly to put the patients' needs first.

Accordingly, discussions with physicians about reorganizing care cannot begin with talk of contracts and compensation. Instead the focus must be squarely on the stakes for patients. Leaders should use data to demonstrate how proposed changes can improve efficiency and patient outcomes and use vignettes about patients' struggles and triumphs to get physicians thinking about what kind of care makes them ashamed or proud. Of course, these discussions must ultimately turn to business issues, but not until patients' welfare is front and center.

Statements of shared purpose, such as the Mayo Clinic's promise that "the needs of the patient come first" and Seattle-based Group Health Cooperative's commitment to "transform health care [by] working together," are effective because they establish an organizational orientation rather than set piecemeal targets. Such statements have three features in common: They are unequivocally focused on patients, they acknowledge that the status quo is inadequate and must change, and they affirm that group action is needed to pursue the shared goal.

Of course, a statement of purpose has little value unless leaders explicitly promote it and put its principles into action. The Cleveland Clinic uses an array of communication tools to reinforce its message of shared purpose. An internal training video developed by the clinic, for example, is a vivid reminder to physicians of the need for empathy and compassion (see the sidebar "Inspiring Shared Purpose").

Sometimes the story of a single patient is enough to galvanize doctors' buy-in. In 2008, for example, a patient called the Cleveland Clinic's urology department seeking an appointment because he was having trouble urinating. He was given the next available slot— two weeks away. A few hours later he arrived in the emergency department with acute urinary retention. Doctors quickly solved the problem, but the patient suffered greatly in the hours before treatment.

The physician leaders discussed the case, and one asked, "Do we want to be the type of organization that doesn't even *try* to figure out if patients should be seen right away?" In that light, the existing appointment system seemed intolerable.

As a result, the clinic instituted a same-day appointment policy whereby all patients who call are asked whether they want to be seen immediately. About one million of the 5.5 million visits a year now occur on the same day the patient calls. This policy occasionally disrupts physicians' schedules, but the new system is comforting to patients, and clinic doctors have come to embrace it. Other providers are now offering similar appointment guarantees.

Another organizational change that supports shared purpose comes from Advocate Health Care in Chicago. In the spring of 2013, senior leaders at Advocate banished all meetings between 8 and 9 AM on weekdays and instituted mandatory "huddles" to discuss safety issues. During the hour, nurses gather on each floor, hospital leaders have their own huddle, and system leaders meet as well to discuss any safety events or near misses. Most of these meetings take just 15 minutes, but if an issue requires investigation, they can fill the hour or go beyond as needed. With the introduction of huddles, reports of serious safety events increased by 40% as staff members embraced leadership's commitment to safety and transparency. Since then, falls and hospital-acquired complications have dramatically decreased. For the first time, six Advocate hospitals have gone at least a year without a central-line-associated bloodstream infection. In a striking vote of confidence in the program, in July 2013 frontline clinicians requested that the safety huddles occur seven days a week, which they now do.

Appealing to Self-Interest

Physicians, like everyone else, are motivated by financial incentives and job security. Even if their organization's noble shared purpose resonates deeply with them, they also care intensely about what measures are being used to gauge their performance and how the data are collected and analyzed. This natural self-interest can be channeled to reinforce engagement in a number of ways.

Some organizations make portions of physicians' compensation dependent upon performance. Pennsylvania-based Geisinger Health System, for example, ties 20% of physicians' potential compensation to their performance against certain goals or, in many cases, on how they do as a team. Cardiac surgeons, for example, are rewarded on the basis of how reliably they perform key processes such as screening steps and the prescription of medications to reduce complications after surgery. Meanwhile, endocrinologists at Geisinger are rewarded if control of glucose levels improves for all diabetes patients, not just those they see. These incentives are designed to reward leadership and collaboration and to inspire everyone to engage in enhancing patient care. In these and other areas, Geisinger has seen substantially improved patient outcomes, including fewer rehospitalizations after cardiac surgery and, for patients with diabetes, reductions in vision loss, heart attacks, and stroke.

Other organizations put physicians on straight salary, believing that all financial incentives can have unintended negative consequences and are an invitation to game the system. The Cleveland Clinic's physicians are all salaried, without any performance-based

Creating Incentives

PHYSICIANS CARE FIRST and foremost about their patients' well-being, but that doesn't mean financial incentives are not of great interest to them as well. This motivational tool can be very effective, especially when the incentives are aligned with the organization's shared purpose. Here are a few strategies for designing effective financial incentives:

Avoid Attaching Large Sums to Any Single Target

It takes a surprisingly small percentage of physicians' compensation to get their attention. We have seen that doctors will focus intensely on improvement targets when as little as 1% of their compensation is at stake. This finding aligns with the behavioral economics principle known as "loss aversion." In essence, people find it more painful to lose something of a given value than they find it agreeable to gain that same value. Thus, doctors typically pay more attention when they stand to lose 1% of income than when they stand to gain it. At Geisinger, where 20% of compensation is based on performance, the incentives are spread across four or more targets.

Watch for Conflicts of Interest

Avoid financial incentives that are focused solely on reducing costs, particularly when the savings are generated by individual physicians' reducing their

---

bonus program. Instead of using overt financial incentives, the clinic hires all physicians on one-year renewable contracts, and they undergo detailed annual performance reviews. The physicians see the yearly reviews not just as a chance to receive feedback but also as an opportunity to communicate with hospital leaders about how the organization could improve. Like Geisinger, the clinic has seen marked improvement in quality and in volume of patients.

Either approach can have sustained effectiveness, we find, but only when used to advance goals that are consistent with shared purpose. If physicians believe that a particular management-endorsed behavior or practice will improve patient care, even minimal financial incentives will be enough to help them implement it consistently. If they are uncertain about whether it will actually improve care, even large incentives will produce only marginal success. (See the sidebar "Creating Incentives.")

use of resources. Such incentives can create real or apparent conflicts of interest when a doctor stands to gain by shortchanging patients. "Gain sharing" programs, in which the organization shares with physicians the savings from improved performance, have not been successful at most hospitals, in part because of their complexity.

Reward Collaboration

Create financial incentives that target outcomes beyond the control of any individual. Physicians (like most people) naturally prefer that their compensation be based on behaviors that they alone control, such as whether they order tests in specific circumstances—but that approach doesn't encourage teamwork.

Communicate

Make sure physicians understand that financial incentives will be continually modified as the organization learns how best to support its shared purpose. This evolution should be transparent and physicians' participation welcomed.

Earning Respect

Nonfinancial rewards and penalties also have a role to play in getting doctors on board. Physicians appreciate positive feedback, and they particularly worry about losing the respect of their colleagues. High-performing organizations are increasingly reporting to physicians how their personal performance compares with that of their colleagues—and providing those data in ways that intensify peer pressure.

Such scrutiny can be excruciating, especially when the data are "unmasked" so that colleagues can see one another's results. Within physician groups at Partners Healthcare System, for example, unmasked data on individual physicians' use of radiology tests led to an almost immediate 10% to 15% drop in orders for high-cost tests, mainly due to decreases among the "outlier" physicians who ordered many more tests than their colleagues. Using peer pressure in this way can achieve cost savings without compromising quality.

Even the physicians who dramatically reduced their use of the tests did not argue that patient care suffered as a result.

Some organizations now post individual physicians' quality-performance data publicly on their websites. Whether consumers are using these data to make decisions is unclear, but doctors, knowing that their performance is on public display, are strongly motivated to improve. University of Utah Health Care used this kind of transparency to improve patient-experience ratings. First, leaders began sharing each physician's patient-experience data with him or her confidentially. Next, they began sharing the data internally so that physicians could see one another's ratings and patient comments. Finally, they began posting the data and comments—good and bad—for every physician on public websites. With each escalation in transparency, overall performance improved. One key to Utah's success with the program, we believe, was its gradual introduction, which allowed physicians to acclimate at each step.

Embracing Tradition

When physicians value membership in an organization—out of pride, a need for security, or some other reason—they are motivated to adhere to that organization's standards and traditions. For example, doctors have followed the Mayo Clinic's dress code since the clinic was founded, in the late 19th century. The requirements today include neckties for men and hosiery for women, even in Mayo's facilities in Arizona, where temperatures routinely top 100°F.

Mayo also has standards for how its physicians communicate with one another (for instance, when paged, they must respond immediately) and how they interact with patients (before out-of-town patients with complex conditions are discharged, physicians must meet with them for "exit" visits to discuss their ongoing care and answer questions). The symbolic connection between the dress code and Mayo's standards for performance is clear: "There is a Mayo way of doing things. Don't come here if you don't want to adopt it—completely." These standards and traditions translate into well-coordinated care that patients appreciate and physicians are proud of. They are also a key reason that Mayo is able to retain many of its students and residents for their entire careers.

Such standards, whether they're related to appearance and etiquette or to the delivery of care, create consistency in the way physicians interact with one another—a basic step toward more-effective teamwork. Even newly minted standards, such as using checklists, can be effective motivators when physicians know that they could be shunned or even lose their jobs if they disregard them.

To successfully use this lever, organizations must be willing to part company with physicians who refuse to work with their colleagues toward a shared purpose. In the past, hospitals welcomed almost any decent physician who could bring in patients (and thus revenue), and doctors hardly ever lost their credentials or were fired. That is still rare, but when it does happen, colleagues usually ask, "What took so long?"

Making It Operational

Most health care organizations already use one or more of the four motivational levers described here. We've found that the most successful rely on all four.

Consider the "full disclosure" initiative launched by Ascension Health, of St. Louis, in 2006. Although the organization believed that communicating openly with patients and families after unexpected events, such as medical errors, was the ethical thing to do, disclosure at Ascension was occurring only 10% of the time. Ascension introduced the program with a reminder about the organization's shared purpose—to put patients first and provide the best possible care. It shared evidence suggesting that full disclosure leads to better outcomes for patients, families, and providers themselves and may reduce malpractice costs. It then focused its implementation efforts on obstetrics, where bad outcomes are particularly emotional, and even more so when they're due to mistakes.

Physicians initially resisted the new policy, worrying that acknowledging errors would lead to malpractice suits despite the evidence to the contrary. Further complicating matters, many of the obstetricians were not employed by Ascension. To overcome resistance, Ascension negotiated premium credits from malpractice insurers for physicians who agreed to full-disclosure training. It also recruited respected local leaders to give talks and use their personal influence to encourage acceptance. And Ascension created a new operational standard: Doctors were required to consult with "event response teams" to address issues that might have been caused by errors. They understood that failure to adhere to this standard could cost them their jobs. In this way, Ascension effectively invoked all four motivational levers: shared purpose (ethical care), self-interest (premium credits), respect (peer pressure), and standards (event response teams).

As a result, Ascension's culture changed with surprising speed. Three months after the protocol's implementation, the disclosure rate for unexpected events rose to 24% percent. A year later it was 41%, and at 27 months it was 53%. Fully 86% of the documented disclosure communications were initiated by the practitioner who had delivered the baby. By pressing all four levers, Ascension had won active engagement from a resistant group of physicians in a challenging new value initiative.

Like Ascension, the emergency department at Brigham and Women's Hospital, in Boston, has used all four motivational levers in a multiyear effort to improve dismal patient-experience ratings. As is true in many emergency departments, the staff initially felt hopeless about its ability to improve patients' experience, because many emergency department patients have mental health issues, face complex socioeconomic challenges, or both. Hospital leaders decided to focus clinicians' attention in a positive direction—on a shared purpose. In one of their first steps, they removed all negative comments from patient-experience surveys and presented clinicians with just the positive ones. Then they asked the clinicians to figure out how to make good patient experiences happen all the time. The goal that emerged was "VIP Care for All."

Of course, the improvement efforts had to go beyond a slogan. The physical layout of the emergency department was streamlined and enlarged. The processes by which patients moved through the

Inspiring Shared Purpose

AT A TIME WHEN STRESS and uncertainty can undermine engagement, leaders need motivational tools to enlist physicians' support and collaboration. A short training video produced by the Cleveland Clinic appeals to clinicians' instinct to put patients' needs first, by inviting staff members to reflect on patients', and one another's, experiences. It asks, "If you could stand in someone else's shoes and feel what they feel, would you treat them differently?" and then shows images of patients in spaces like a hospital, in a waiting room, and in an elevator, with words describing their thoughts: "Daughter is getting married on Saturday—determined to be there." "They saw 'something' on her mammogram." "Just found out he's going to be a dad." A vivid reminder of the power of empathy and compassion, the video encourages physicians to embrace health care's higher purpose.

emergency department were redesigned after an intensive "lean management" study. Dashboards were developed to enable doctors to see how their performance compared with that of their colleagues on measures such as patients' length of stay (door-to-discharge or -admission times), patient-experience data, and number of visits. Standards were set governing how clinicians should work together, and leaders made it clear that adherence was not optional. Financial incentives rewarded improvement for both individuals and groups of clinicians.

The changes were dramatic and sustained. Door-to-bed time improved from 65 minutes in 2009 to 22 minutes in 2013, and more than half of emergency department patients are now in beds within nine minutes of arrival. "Walkouts" declined from 3.3% to 1.5%. And patient satisfaction rose from the 6th percentile to as high as the 99th percentile, remaining above the 90th percentile during most quarters since the effort began.

Transformation of health care requires the will to organize delivery around the needs of patients—and that reorientation means the end of the status quo and doctors' traditional perch within it. Clearly, getting physicians' buy-in to this strategic change will be hard, particularly from those who have long practiced under the old regime. Many organizations are cultivating "farm teams"—developing training programs that emphasize team-based, patient-centered care and then recruiting the graduates.

But health care leaders cannot wait for generations of physicians to retire from the scene. Engaging doctors, even the old guard, is a management challenge that can be tackled, measured, and improved. The organizations that can help physicians to live up to their aspirations as caregivers—to understand that giving up their autonomy is not actually surrender but a noble act of humility in the interest of their patients—will be the ones that improve efficiency, deliver the best outcomes, increase their market share, and retain and recruit the best people.

Originally published in June 2014. Reprint R1406H

About the Contributors

DEBORAH ANCONA is the Seley Distinguished Professor of Management at MIT's Sloan School of Management.

MARCIA BLENKO is a partner at Bain & Company in Boston and leads Bain's Global Organization practice.

JIM COLLINS operates a management research laboratory in Boulder, Colorado.

TOBY COSGROVE, MD, is the CEO of the Cleveland Clinic.

PETER F. DRUCKER was a professor of social science and management at Claremont Graduate University in California.

AMY C. EDMONDSON is the Novartis Professor of Leadership and Management at Harvard Business School and the author of *Teaming: How Organizations Learn, Innovate, and Compete in the Knowledge Economy* (Jossey-Bass, 2012).

DANIEL GOLEMAN cochairs the Consortium for Research on Emotional Intelligence in Organizations at Rutgers University.

RONALD A. HEIFETZ codirects the Center for Public Leadership at Harvard University's Kennedy School of Government.

ROBERT S. KAPLAN is the Baker Foundation Professor at Harvard Business School and codeveloper, with David P. Norton, of the balanced scorecard.

JOHN P. KOTTER is the Konosuke Matsushita Professor of Leadership, Emeritus, at Harvard Business School.

DONALD L. LAURIE is a founder and managing partner at Oyster International, a Boston-based consulting firm.

THOMAS H. LEE, MD, is the chief medical officer at Press Ganey and the former network president of Partners HealthCare.

THOMAS W. MALONE is the Patrick J. McGovern Professor of Management at MIT's Sloan School of Management.

JAMES I. MERLINO is a colorectal surgeon and the chief experience officer at the Cleveland Clinic.

DAVID P. NORTON is the founder and president of the Balanced Scorecard Collaborative, Palladium Group, in Massachusetts.

WANDA J. ORLIKOWSKI is the Eaton-Peabody Professor of Communication Sciences at MIT's Sloan School of Management.

ANANTH RAMAN is the UPS Foundation Professor of Business Logistics at Harvard Business School.

PAUL ROGERS is managing partner for the United Kingdom at Bain & Company's London office.

PETER M. SENGE is a senior lecturer at MIT's Sloan School of Management.

Index

empowerment, 49
engagement, 198, 199–209
executives, effective, 23–36
external motivation, 15

failure, embracing, 111
family businesses, 27–28
feedback, 157, 159, 161, 173–177
figurative scaffolding, 106–107
financial measures, 156, 157
financial pressures, vii
financial rewards
    linking to performance measures,
        168, 170
    for physicians, 203–205
Ford, Henry, 149

Gault, Stanley C., 72–73
Geisinger Health System, 198, 203
Gerstner, Lou, 46–47
Gillette, 65–68
globalization, 18–19, 137–138
global markets, 124–127, 138
goal setting, 167–168
Goleman, Daniel, 1–22
Group Danone, 113
Grove, Andy, 151

health care
    costs, viii
    engaging doctors in transforma-
        tion of, 197–210
    improving, vii–viii
    operational standards, 207–209
    quality of, vii, 179–195
    shared purpose in, 200–203
    traditions, 206–207
health care leaders
    path to leadership for, 38

role of, viii
transformation of, vii–viii
health care providers
    See also doctors
    patient experience and, 181–195
    pride and confidence in organiza-
        tion of, 2
    role of, vii
hedgehog concept, 61, 67
Heifetz, Ronald A., 79–100
high-level perspective, 81–84
hiring process, self-awareness in, 9
holding environment, 86–87
humility, 59, 60, 65–70, 76

Iacocca, Lee, 69–70
IDEO, 143
impulsive behavior, 12, 14
incentive systems, 168, 170, 203–205
incomplete leaders, 137–154
informal relationship networks, 53
information economy, 19
information flow, 31–32
inquiring, 143–145
inspired standards, 60, 70–71
integrated delivery systems, 118
integrity, 14
interdependence, 46–48, 107–109
internal motivation, 15–17
inventing, 138, 141, 149–153
Iverson, Ken, 74

J. Lyons & Company, 28
Jobs, Steve, 151
John Lewis, 131–132
Johnson, Earvin "Magic," 81–82

Kaplan, Robert S., 155–178
Kelleher, Herb, 151

Engage with HBR content the way you want, on any device.

With HBR's subscription plans, you can access world-renowned case studies from Harvard Business School and receive four **free eBooks**. Download and customize prebuilt **slide decks and graphics** from our **Data & Visuals** collection. With HBR's archive, top 50 best-selling articles, and five new articles every day, HBR is more than just a magazine.

Subscribe Today
HBR.org/success

Harvard
Business
Review

The most important management ideas all in one place.

We hope you enjoyed this book from *Harvard Business Review*. Now you can get even more with HBR's 10 Must Reads Boxed Set. From books on leadership and strategy to managing yourself and others, this 6-book collection delivers articles on the most essential business topics to help you succeed.

HBR's 10 Must Reads Series

The definitive collection of ideas and best practices on our most sought-after topics from the best minds in business.

- Change Management
- Collaboration
- Communication
- Emotional Intelligence
- Innovation
- Leadership
- Making Smart Decisions

- Managing Across Cultures
- Managing People
- Managing Yourself
- Strategic Marketing
- Strategy
- Teams
- The Essentials

hbr.org/mustreads

Buy for your team, clients, or event.
Visit hbr.org/bulksales for quantity discount rates.